I0425474

Black Nation
Mother and Father Of Civilization

by
Rasheed L. Muhammad
(Formerly known as Anthony L. Muhammad)

This Book is dedicated to Minister Louis Farrakhan.
It was from one of his luminous lectures I heard in
Philadelphia wherein his words enriched me
to write about the subject matter
contained in this
book.

Copyright © 2009 All Rights Reserved

First Edition 1997
(Original Title)
Mysteries of the Bible, Quran and Minister Louis Farrakhan Revealed in Black and White

Second Edition 2010
(New Title)
Black Nation Mother and Father of Civilization Africa

Third Edition 2013

Table of Contents

FORWARD

Because this book covers thousands of years of history, I thought it best to provide a letter written by Elijah Muhammad in 1936 regarding the importance of history.

DEPARTMENT OF SUPREME WISDOM
April 2, 1936

First: History is all our studies. The most attractive and best qualified to reward our research. As it develops the springs and motives of human action, and displays the consequence of circumstances which operates most powerfully on the destinies of human beings.

Second: It stands true that we the Lost Found NATION, of ISLAM, in the wilderness of North America have not applied ourselves to the study of History. But rather to FOLLY having a lots of the bread of, idleness and when an effort was made to the above affect of History study, it was to our detriment by not knowing what History that was more valuable, to aid us in the knowledge of our own Nation.

The WISE MAN, is the one who has made a careful study of the Past events of ANCIENT and MODERN HISTORY. The KNOWLEDGE of the FUTURE is JUDGED by the

KNOWLEDGE of the PAST. There are MEN born with a gift of PROPHECY. While some are trained into the KNOWLEDGE by intense studies of the PAST EVENTS OF HISTORY...

By Elijah Mohammad
Servant of Allah

CHAPTER 1

Golgotha

When you look at the shape of the African continent you'll see the profile of a human skull. When I came to see more deeply into the geographical contour and interior of the skull shaped African continent, it moved me to research the various functions of the human brain. What I discovered was astounding. The brain is theoretically divided into areas referred to as pre-frontal, frontal, parietal, temporal, occipital and cerebellum. When I lay a diagram of the human brain onto the African skull shaped continent, they seem to fit perfectly as shown throughout the pages of this book.

According to the Christian bible, Golgotha means: The place of the skull. The bible says of Golgotha, *"And they bring him unto the place Golgotha, which is, being interpreted, the place of the skull. And they gave him to drink wine mingled with myrrh: but he received it not. And when they had crucified him, they parted his garments, casting lots upon them, what every man should take."* (Mark 15:22-24) Could it also be that Golgotha represents Africa and its ancient people who were torn apart through war and Colonialization? It is my belief that a compelling fulfillment of the above biblical passage occurred during the 1880's when European powers scrambled to steal Africa's resources. When Europe seized upon Africa's resources and"*they parted his (Africa) garments (resources), casting lots upon them, what every man (European power) should take"* Europe fulfilled *Biblical Mark 15:22-24*.

The Scramble for Africa also known as the Race for Africa was the proliferation of conflicting European claims to African territory during the "New Imperialism period." The last 20 years of the 19th century saw the transition from "informal imperialism" of control through military influence and economic dominance to that of direct rule. Attempts to mediate imperial competition, such as the Berlin Conference (1884-1885) between Britain, France and Germany, failed to establish definitively the competing powers' claims.

The Berlin Conference of 1884–85 regulate d European colonization and trade in Africa during the New Imperialism period, and coincided with Germany's sudden emergence as an imperial power. Called for by Portugal and organized by Otto von Bismarck, the first Chancellor of Germany, its outcome, the General Act of the Berlin Conference, is often seen as the formalization of the Scramble for Africa. The conference ushered in a period of heightened colonial activity on the part of the European powers, while simultaneously eliminating most existing forms of African autonomy and self-governance.[1]

Political tampering with the land and ancient people of Africa by European powers played a major role into its present woes. Since then, Africa has been under the influence of a diabolical rule and scheme of an evil child-like mind. Until this day, her declaration of independence, since the 1950's, has not freed Africa from the damage of European mischief making viz., colonialization thus their body politic is yet in disrepair.

1884 The Berlin Conference (Werner)

---

[1] http://en.wikipedia.org/wiki/Berlin_Conference#Early_history_of_the_conference

Did the wickedly wise political and religious scientists of Europe know of Africa's geo-scriptural connection as Golgotha? It is my belief *"The Berlin Conference of 1884"* represented the straw that broke Africa's back. When European governmental powers decided to officially organize to divide Africa, their crucifixion and ultimate geopolitical death was sealed for a season and for a reason. However, on another degree of understanding, there were other initial forces at play that caused Africa's original inhabitants to become separated and set asunder. Those forces of which I speak are called forces of division. These forces produced continental globe movements or tectonic plate movements.

> *"The main force that shapes our planet's surface over long amounts of time is the movement of Earth's outer layer by the process of plate tectonics.*
>
> *"These plates are made of rock, but the rock is, in general, lightweight compared with the denser, fluid layer underneath. This allows the plates to "float" on top of the denser material.*
>
> *"Movements deep within the Earth, which carry heat from the hot interior to the cooler surface, cause the plates to move very slowly on the surface, about 2 inches per year. There are several different hypotheses to explain exactly how these motions allow plates to move.*
>
> *"Interesting things happen at the edges of plates. Subduction zones form when plates crash into each other, spreading ridges form when plates pull away from each other, and large faults form when plates slide past each other."[2]*

Our earth's plate movements actually forebode that a new people would ultimately rule the globe through a force of division because every physical law has an equal spiritual law—the cause and effect theory. Therefore, as the physical plates of our globe were changing and moving into different locations, it

---

[2] http://www.windows.ucar.edu/tour/link=/earth/interior/plate_tectonics.html

served as a spiritual sign of what humanity might expect to come to pass among civilization processes.

Ancient Greeks once taught that the Earth was a supercontinent—one. They called it Pangaea. (See Illustration I)

Illustration I

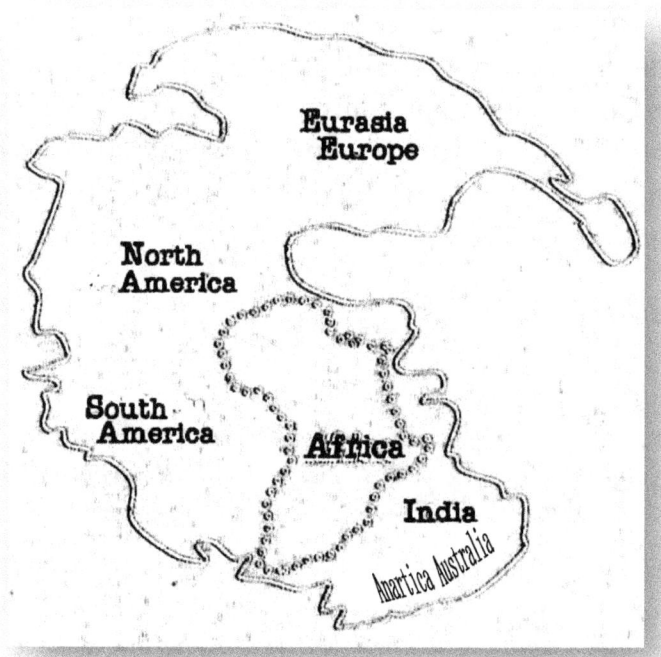

According to modern geologists, this is how the land of the Earth appeared when it was a supercontinent—Pangaea. If you use your imagination, Pangaea may remind you of a fetus of sorts.

> *"Pangaea, name given the single supercontinent that existed on Earth during the late Paleozoic and early Mesozoic eras (about 300 million to 200 million years ago). Pangaea was made up of two connected continental masses: Gondwanaland to the south and Laurasia to the north. The modern continents are the result of the breakup of Pangaea, followed by the breakup of Gondwanaland and Laurasia. The processes that formed Pangaea and later broke it apart are known as plate tectonics, sometimes called continental drift.*

"The name Pangaea (Greek for "all land") was coined in 1912 by Alfred Wegener, the German meteorologist who published the first scientifically argued theory of continental drift. Utilizing geological and fossil evidence, Wegener postulated the existence of Pangaea as a supercontinent that had existed throughout the early history of Earth."[3]

Planet earth's present form certainly make it obvious that a force of division has caused a separation of one land mass into the many continents we see today thus shaping the Mother continent, Africa, into the profile of a human skull. Of course, it took trillions of years to form and reform our globe into its current appearance with much pain to all life on earth. I imagine her pain also affected the human brain, psychology and civilization along the will of time.

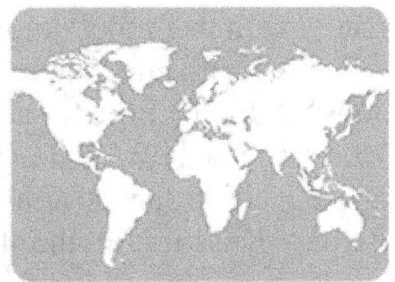

Europe Learned From Africa

Long before Europe's so-called mission to civilize Africa, Africa had already shown its genius. Some of its great civilizations, such as Kush, Axum, Ghana, Mali, and Great Zimbabwe had flourished and many major scientific advances were known in Africa long before Europe's age of enlightenment. For instance, towards the middle of the 12th century, the North African scientist, Al Idrisi, wrote, *"What results from the opinion of philosophers, learned men and those skilled in observation of the heavenly bodies, is that the world is as round as a sphere, of which the waters are adherent and maintained upon its surface by natural equilibrium."* Africans were certainly involved in trans-oceanic travel long before Europeans and there is some evidence to suggest that Africans crossed the Atlantic and reached the American continent, perhaps even North America, as early as 500 BC.

---

[3] http://encarta.msn.com/encyclopedia_761586400/Pangaea.html

In the 14th century, the Syrian writer, al-Umari, wrote about the voyage of the Emperor of Mali who crossed the Atlantic with 2000 ships but failed to return. Africans in east and southeastern Africa also set up great civilizations that established important trading links with the kingdoms and empires of India and China long before Europeans had learned how to navigate the Atlantic Ocean. When Europeans first sailed to Africa in the 15th century, African pilots and navigators shared with them their knowledge of Trans-oceanic travel.

African knowledge and that of the ancient world, was transmitted to Europe as a result of the North African or Moorish conquest of the Iberian peninsular in the 8th century. There were in fact several such conquests including two by the Berber dynasties in the 11th and 12th centuries. The Muslim invasion of Europe, and the founding of the state of Cordoba, re-introduced all the learning of the ancient world as well as the various contributions made by Islamic scholars and linked Europe much more closely with North and West Africa. Arabic numerals based on those used in India were introduced and they helped simplify mathematical calculations.

Europe was also introduced to the learning of the ancient world mainly through Arabic translations of works in the fields of medicine, chemistry, astronomy, mathematics and philosophy. So important was the knowledge found in Muslim Spain, that one Christian monk - Adelard of Bath - disguised himself as a Muslim in order to study at the university at Cordoba. Many historians believe that it was this knowledge, brought to Europe through Muslim Spain, which not only created the conditions for the Renaissance but also for the eventual expansion of Europe overseas in the 15th century.[4]

---

[4] www.antislavery.org/breakingthesilence/main/briefings/1.%20Africa%20before%20the%20Transatlantic%20Slave%20Trade.doc

This map demonstrates a timeline showing only a few ancient institutionalized Original civilizations that existed long before Europe evolved its many world-class nation states.

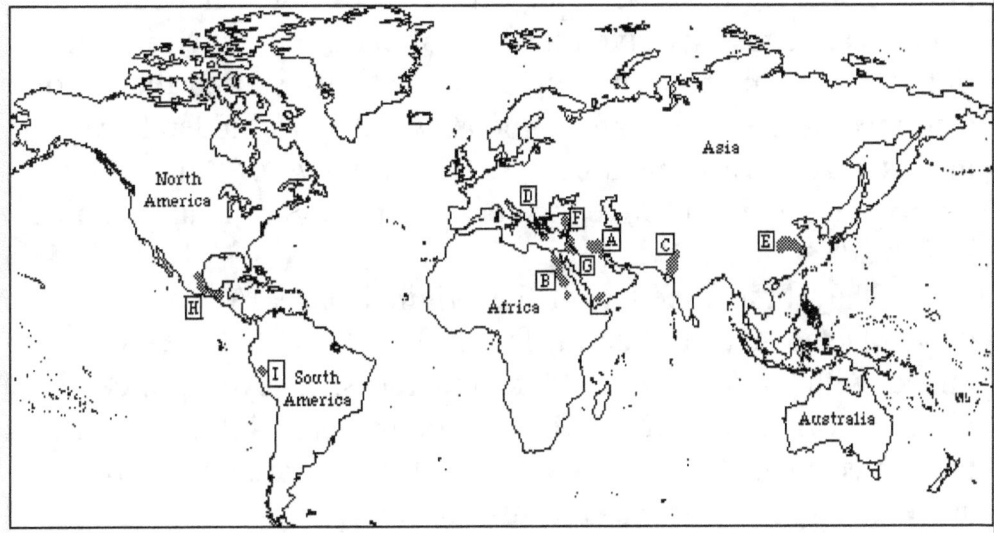

History 370: Ancient History
Map #1--Early World Civilizations

A = Sumerian Civilization (ca. 3500 B. C.) -- Later Akkadian, Babylonian, Assyrian, Chaldian, Persian...

B = Egyptian Civilization (ca. 3000 B. C.) -- Later Nubian, Kushitic, and Ethiopic.

C = Indus Valley Civilization (ca. 2500 B. C.) -- Later Indian civilization (Aryan, Mauryan, Guptan)

D = Minoan Civilization (ca. 2500 B. C.) -- Later Mycenean, Hellenic, and Hellenistic.

E = Wei and Shang China (ca. 1500 B.C.) -- Later Chinese dynasties (Chou, Chin, Han)

F= Hittite Civilization (ca. 1500 B. C.) -- Later Anatolian civilization (Lydian, Phrygian, Caria, etc.)

G= Canaanite Civilization (ca. 1500 B. C.) -- Later Phoenician, Israelitic, Carthaginian, etc.

H = Olmec Civilization (ca. 1200 B. C.) -- Later Mesoamerican Civilization (Toltec, Mayan, Aztec)

I = Chavin Civilization (ca. 900 B. C.) -- Later Andean civilization (Chimu, Inca, etc.)

[Source]: www.uncp.edu/home/

The Honorable Elijah Muhammad taught the Black Man originally inhabited the earth, families to themselves. Later on as color (brown yellow, red) began among them by the original scientists (says the word of Allah to me) they became families to themselves, and from families to tribes: the term used today is "races" or "nations."

Most of the blacks remained in the East along and below the equator of the earth. The white race, after their creation 6,000 years ago, was given the part of earth today that is called Europe. It is this race of people who actually started the sin of race-mixing[5] the two strange bloods, which is forbidden by God; just as they have disregarded all Divine Laws of Allah (God). They even seem to change the very natural law of man in which he is made.

They first mixed with the original black Arabs then, as they traveled over the earth, for the past near 500 years, they mixed with brown, yellow and red races. They captured the blacks and made slaves of them. For the past 400 years, they have used them (so-called Negroes) for experimental purposes and even use them now as one uses his tool![6]

---

[5] physiognomical
[6] www.muhammadspeaks.com/thetruth4-5-1962.htmlgovernment for self ?

CHAPTER 2

Africa is Geographical Brain

Africa is a geographical brain map, as I see it, and its original ancient inhabitants once carried out a divine function from which they served and educated all of humanity by putting pen to paper and stone revealing wisdom, knowledge and understanding. *"And We [نَحْنُ nahnu] did not send you except as a mercy to the world."(Holy Quran 21:107)* The Mother continent and her people should be seen as a people operating in the brain of the globe.

Africa and the Holy Land (geographical brain map's prefrontal cortex) were once connected. The prefrontal cortex is situated at the foremost section of the brain where the holy land is fixed. (See Illustration II) It is responsible for the executive functions, which include mediating conflicting thoughts, making choices between right and wrong or good and bad, predicting future events, and governing social control -- such as suppressing emotional or sexual urges. The pre-frontal cortex is the brain center most strongly implicated in qualities like human general intelligence, and personality. When the pathways between the prefrontal cortex and the rest of the brain are damaged due to head injury, massive personality changes can result. One might say that the prefrontal cortex is the neurological basis of the <u>conscience</u>. Weak interconnections between the prefrontal cortex and the rest of the brain have been observed in criminals, socio-paths, drug addicts, and schizophrenics.

The prefrontal cortex is fed information from all the senses, and combines this information to form useful judgments. It constantly contains active representation in working memory, as well as representation of goals and contexts. Unfortunately, the pre-frontal cortex, one of the most important areas in the brain, is also one of the most susceptible to injury.[7]

Illustration II

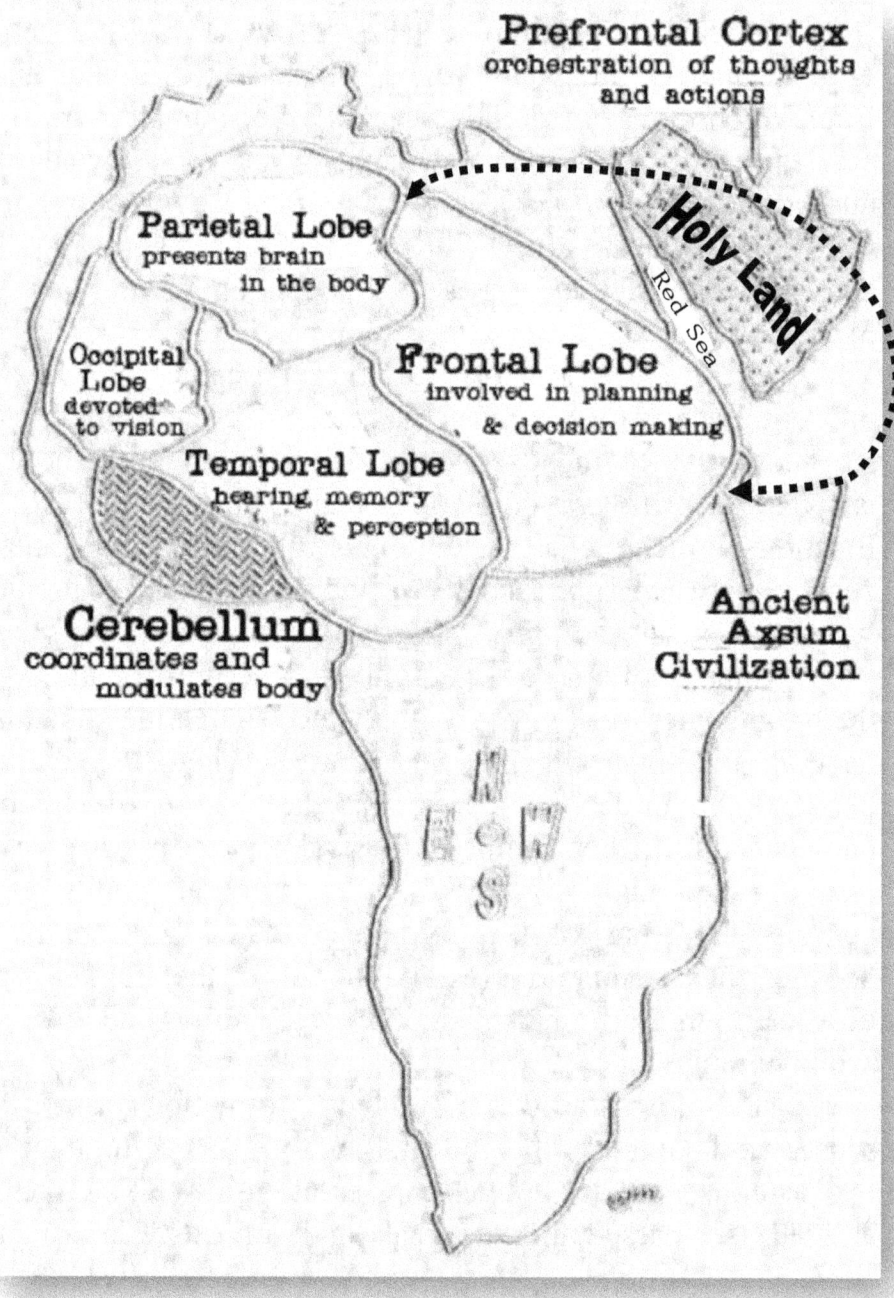

[7] http://www.wisegeek.com/what-is-the-prefrontal-cortex.htm

There is no question about the historical and religious significance of the holy land. Numerous prophets of God and great Kings and Queens were produced within this region of the globe. When one speaks to what Prophet Abraham brought, we think about the three great religions namely Judaism, Christianity and Islam. *"Abraham"* is often viewed as the father of all three of these chief faiths. We know he labored in the holy land as a theological figure - traditionally 2000 BCE -1500 BCE. However, today far too many religious believers who claim Abraham have gone religiously mad, criminal, sociopathic, and schizophrenic. They seem unable to neither establish peace or assign priorities for peace nor make balanced decisions as to when to accept peace. But more importantly, none can decide how to share WEALTH—the root of evil deeds!

When we read news about what is happening in the Middle East and/or holy land in general, there are certainly massive personality changes between them and what we typically perceive as holy people. Death is being bred as if no prophet or messenger has ever set foot in that region. What separates Africa from the holy land today is the Red Sea (that is Suez Canal), which I refer to as a lesion. This lesion between the motherland and the holy land represents damage to her frontal lobes.

The countries across the Red Sea, west of the holy land, are Egypt, Sudan, Ethiopia, Somalia, and Ancient Axsum. These countries are situated in the frontal lobe region of the geographical brain map. Today suffering is either due to war, corruption, starvation, or near extinction. With regard to geographical frontal lobe damage, let us take a lesson from what occurred in east Africa's ancient empire called Aksum or Axsum—Ethiopia.

"Axsum or Aksum Empire was the 3rd largest African empire at 1.25 million sq km. In the sixth century, the kingdom of <u>Aksum</u> (Axum) was doing what many elsewhere had been doing: pursuing trade and empire. Despite the disintegration of the Roman Empire in the 400's

19

and the decline in world trade, Aksum's trade increased during that century. Its exports of ivory, glass crystal, brass and copper items, and perhaps slaves, among other things, had brought prosperity to the kingdom. Some people had become wealthy and cosmopolitan. Aksum's port city on the Red Sea, Adulis, bustled with activity. Its agriculture and cattle breeding flourished, and Aksum extended its rule to Nubia, across the Red Sea to Yemen, and it had extended its rule to the northern Ethiopian Highlands and along the coast to Cape Guardafui.

"From Aksum's beginnings in the third century, Christianity there had spread. But at the peak of Christianity's success, Aksum began its decline. In the late 600s, Aksum's trade was diminished by the clash between Constantinople and the Sassanid Empire. The Sassanid Empire clashed with Constantinople over trade on the Red Sea and expanded into Yemen, driving Aksum out of Arabia. Then Islam united Arabia and began expanding. In the 700's, Muslims occupied the Dahlak Islands just off the coast of Adulis, which had been ruled by Aksum. The Muslims moved into the port city of Adulis, and Aksum's trade by sea.

"Aksum was now cut off from much of the world. Greek- the language of trade - declined there. Minted coins became rare. Paganism revived and mixed with Christianity. And it has been surmised that the productivity of soil in the area was being diminished by over-exploitation and the cutting down of trees. Taking advantage of Aksum's weakness, the Bedja people, who had been living just north of Aksum, moved in. The people of Aksum, in turn, migrated into the Ethiopian Highlands, where they overran small farmers and settled at <u>Amhara,</u> among other nearby places. And with this migration a new Ethiopian civilization began".[8]

As you can see, war upset the balance of power for this ancient African civilization. (Review Illustration II) It appears ancient Axsum's trouble began in the East. Therefore, I reiterate, in neurological terms, frontal lobe damage induces erratic behavior and points to a disease in the frontal limbic connections when tiny charges in the physical, chemical and electrical state of the brain cause shifts in behavior…damage to the frontal

---

[8] http://africankingdoms.com/

lobes can [also] bring about chemical imbalances at far distant sites within the brain.[9]

In terms of Sudan, also located in the frontal lobe region of the geographical brain map, the Fur people live mostly in the Sudan, in Darfur province, named for them. Fur oral tradition attributes ancient ruins [of Sudan] to a mysterious people called the  Torra. After the Torra, the Daju ruled the area, based in Jebel Marra, then the Tunjur, based in Dar Furnung.

The images you see above are some of the ruins built by ancient Black men and women of Sudan (ancient Nubia) within our [g]lobes frontal lobe area. Overall, the ancient people of Sudan have a long history extending from antiquity, which is intertwined with the history of ancient Egypt, with which it was united politically over several periods. However, during these modern times, Sudan is ranked as the second most politically unstable country in the world according to the Failed States Index, for its military dictatorship and the ongoing humanitarian crisis in Darfur.[10] I reiterate, in neurological terms, when the frontal lobes are damaged or destroyed, a person's ability to synthesize signals from the environment, assign priorities, or make balanced decisions is impaired…and the limbic system is free to fire its message of emotions. [1]

In essence, the damage that has occurred in East Africa, the Middle East and the holy land has had far reaching negative affects across the entire globe.

As man is created from the dust of the earth, the geographical changes made to the earth were but a sign that its

---

[9] The Brain, by Dr. Richard Rastak: pg. 152
[10] http://en.wikipedia.org/wiki/Sudan

people would not escape what "Mother Earth" underwent. Its changes were too somehow affecting the physiological changes of the human mind and thus civilization. After all, people are forces too and must mature and expand until we gain balance, which often time occurs in old age.

Once again, our globes geographical changes predicted the spiritual changes that ultimately set the tone for man's political climate. In other words, material matter produces spiritual changes that manifest its symptoms through the socio-political realm of civilization.

Effectively the lesion between the holy land and the motherland overall geographically foretold of the problems that man's civilization would experience. How it was going to become erratic, off-balanced, ill formed and handicapped but only for a reason and for a reason.

The original civilizations' of the Black nation were the first to fall victim to erratic behavior and judgment impairment. They were the first to rule the East—holy land, the first to receive divine scripture and prophets. After the fall, then came separate religions, governments and warfare.

> *"A religious war is a war caused by religious differences. It can involve one state with an established religion against another state with a different religion or a different sect within the same religion, or a religiously motivated group attempting to spread its faith by violence, or to suppress another group because of its religious beliefs or practices. The Muslim Conquests, the French Wars of Religion, the Crusades, and the Reconquista are frequently cited historical examples.*

> *"The Muslim concept of Jihad, or Holy War was set down in the 7th Century. Saint Augustine is credited as being the first to detail a "Just War" theory within Christianity, whereby war is justifiable on religious grounds. Saint Thomas Aquinas elaborated on these criteria and his writings were used by the Roman Catholic Church to regulate the actions of European countries*

> *In the Jewish religion, the expression Milhemet Mitzvah (Hebrew: " מלחמת מצווה, commandment war") refers to a war that is both*

obligatory for all Jews (men and women) and limited to within the borders of the land of Israel.[11]

All war unfortunately is somehow fought over the control of what our globe produces. Man has not yet matured enough to devise a way to share and to properly distribute and trade earth resources—WEALTH! When this is achieved, universal peace may reign supreme.

---

[11] http://en.wikipedia.org/wiki/Religious_war

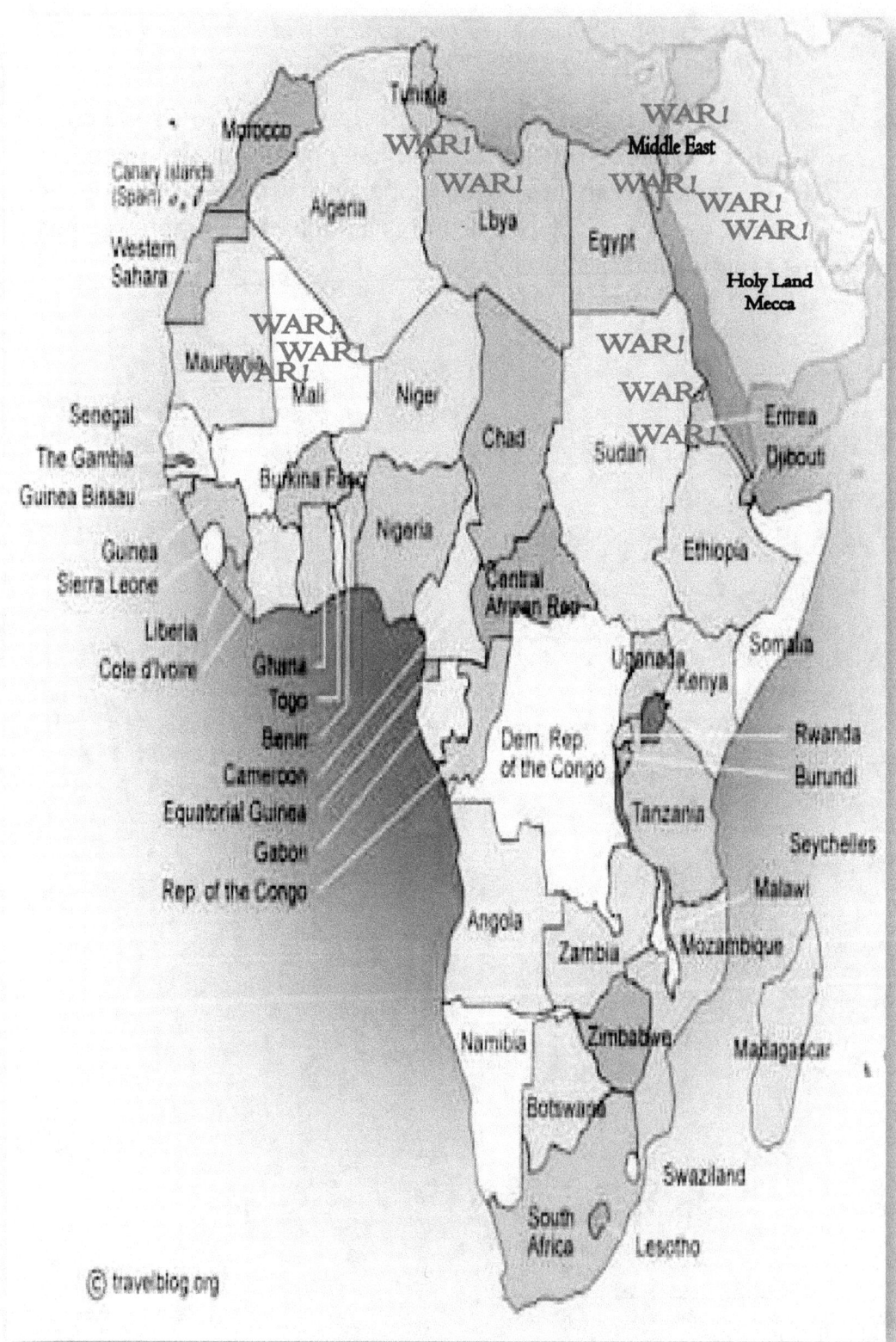

CHAPTER 3

Fall of Original Black Nation

So far we have read what happens when damage occurs in the prefrontal cortex and frontal lobe regions of the brain. This damage can also parallel to what has happened with the words of major prophet's whom were all born, inspired and qualified in the east and Middle East. Such prophets were like conduits delivering God's message via the scriptures to both man and mankind. Over time, as their words from the scriptures reached far distances across the globe, many changes and arrangements were made to the original scripts. These scripts have come to be known as Torah, Injil (old/new Testament) and Quran—the purest of the previous two. Millions upon millions of so-called adherents of each of these scripts are yet divided and conflicted. Thus they have damaged many human beings and family relationships that have produced mental anguish in the name of a religion or a prophet.

Some prophets were Black skin, some Brownish-Red skin and others olive skin. Whatever the case, one of the greatest prophets of all time who had his roots tied directly into the original Black inhabitants of Arabia is Mohammed Ibn Abdullah, the last Arabian prophet sent to mankind. His Divine work took place in what I describe as the geographical Prefrontal Lobe of the [g]lobe. (See Illustration III)

More scholarly evidence will be represented to authenticate that Black skin people were the Original people on earth and therefore the first people of the holy land—Mecca, Arabia.

*"In the most ancient records the whole Arabia was commonly designed under the generic name of "**Kush**", which was extended throughout the entire region comprised between Southern Mesopotamia in the north and the White Nile Basin in the south, that is, including both sides of the Red Sea and the Gulf of Aden. Subsequently, there has been a clear distinction between Northern*

and Southern Arabia since early times, distinction that endured for centuries. The Arabs are the result of the progressive fusion of both entities developed over the original Kushite background."[12]

European writers define the <u>Kingdom of Kush</u> as an ancient nation in northeastern Africa comprising large areas within present-day Egypt and Sudan. The Bible refers to them as Cush meaning "Dark". According to Genesis, Cush's other sons were <u>Seba</u>, <u>Havilah</u>, <u>Sabtah</u>, <u>Raamah</u>, and <u>Sabtecah</u>, names identified by modern scholars with Arabian tribes.

Illustration III

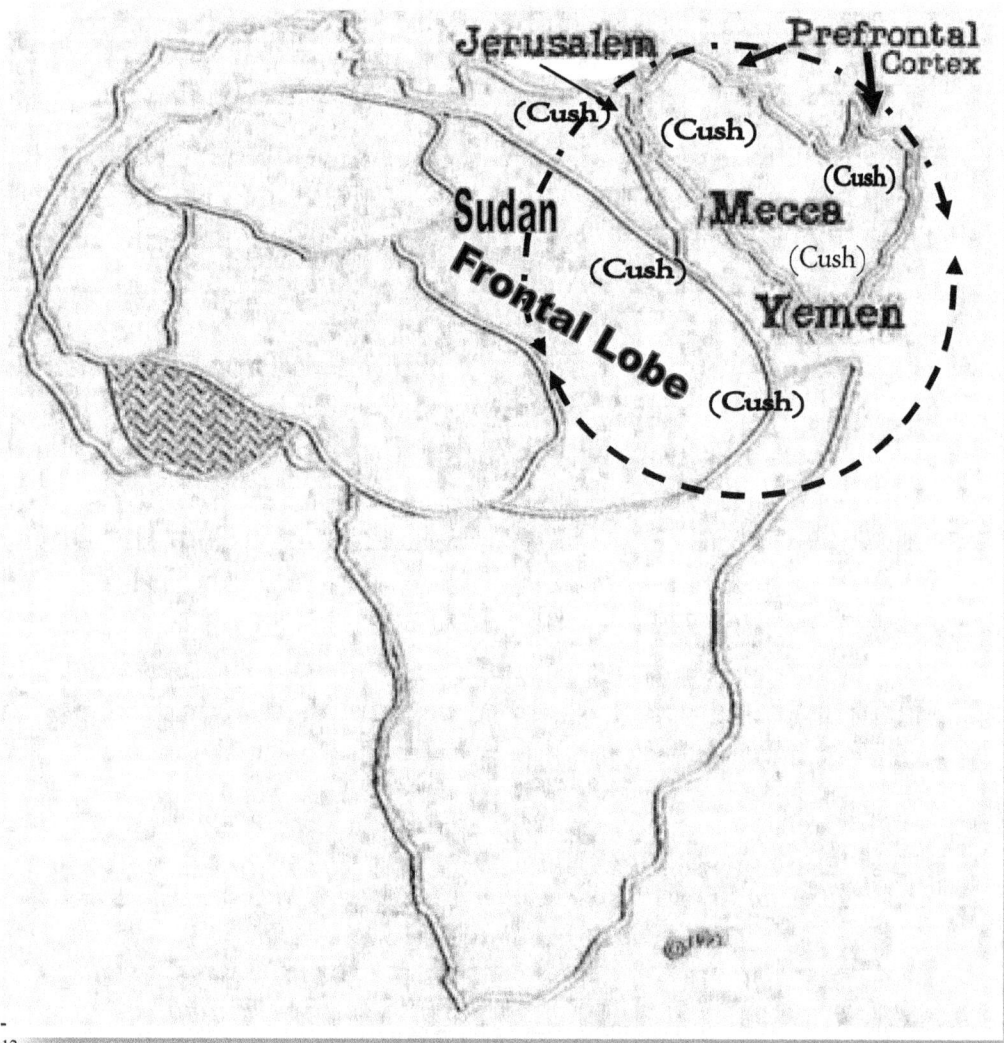

---

[12] http://www.imninalu.net/myths-Arabs.htm

Early in the history of the Black Arabian families of Koryesh (ca. 400 CE) is a character of substantial notoriety. His name was Qusai and it was because of this prior lineage that the Black Koryesh became the ancestral guardians of the Sacred Black Stone of the Kaaba and the most powerful tribe in their valley homeland that included Mecca…He persuaded Quarish to build houses around the Kaaba…Undoubtedly, it was the Black Arabian families that lived close to the Kaaba and the Red Semites who were ostracized. This seems to be the cause of the separation with the Koryesh, which cause great resentment and malignity between the Black Koryesh and the Semites, who would later become the powerful Umayyad or Ummeyyah…Qusai is both the common ancestor of the final Muslim Prophet, Mohammed Ibn Abdullah and the Umayyad family. [2]

As you see, a separation was in the making between two major tribes (families) in the holy land. Consequently, within 50 years after the obvious establishment of the religion of Islam, the Umayyad tribe officially established their own Islamic of capital in Damascus, Syria over a dispute they had with one of Prophet Mohammed's cousins viz., Ali. So here again another separation—a religious war of sorts occurred in the East. Ironically, this is how Sunni and Shia Muslim precincts came to birth. Unfortunately to create these two groups, warfare among the early Islamic nation of 1,400 years ago ignited in the holy land—geographical Prefrontal Lobe—after the death of the last Arabian Prophet, Muhammad Ibn Abdullah (peace be upon him).

Trouble in the holy land is definitely connected to a physical law operating beneath our globe. Nothing could prevent its division. Division came with the first motion of the Creator-God of the Universe. His first movement created another world order from nothing into something. The Self-Created God evolved and developed by His force and will of movement to create division among all particles yet regulated by ONE centrifugal law. In a word or two, this was a conflict between the law of motion and the law of inertia.

> *"Behold! in the creation of the heavens and the earth, and the alternation of Night and Day,— there are indeed Signs for men of understanding. Men who celebrate the praises of Allah standing, sitting, and lying down on their sides, and contemplate the (wonders of) creation in the heavens and the earth, (with the thought): "our Lord! you have not created (all) this without meaning and purpose, Limitless are you in your glory."' (Quran 3:190-191)*

Semites verses Blacks

Gradually many of the Semitic Arabs were compelled to surrender to the wisdom and cultural superiority of their Black neighbors and were forced to adhere to the Yemenite LAW and adapt Yemenite language and custom. Some subversive factions chafed under foreign rule and were a source of social unrest and upheaval. In time through as portion of the Semites became an integral part of the cultural fabric of this mixed Arab society. The gradual amalgamation of these Red Arabs with the original Black Arabs produced a more culturally refined and civilized Semite. This physiognomical blending also resulted in the development of a darker skinned Semite with a slender yet muscular build. Uthman Amr Ibn Bahr Al-Jahiz, renowned Islamic, 'in 860 CE commented on this race mixing: [said], When they [Blacks] mixed with our group, they were said to be tan and brownish-black…and their name was derived from ours, at a time when we were the only ones to be called Blacks. They [Semites] must not be called Blacks unless they are from us'. The debut of this dark Semite on the Arabian stage caused a change in 'attitude toward the Blacks who had led them from the darkness of barbarism into the light of civilization. Such is the testimony of the historians in antiquity: *'The Semitic Arabs take pride in blackness of color'*…This new perspective on black was not held by all Semitic Arab tribes and families; many chose to remain *'in cultural stagnation to live and die by the sword'*. This group of Semitics continued to look upon the Arabian Blacks with distain and malice.

The next change in the relations between Arabian Blacks and Red Semitics was a result of another pivotal population shift. Black families in the north began to return to their ancestral homes in Yemen and the balance of power rotated again from north to south. The northern Black fortifications were weakened and, eventually, the Semites gained control in the early sixth century and, putting into practice what they had learned from the Yemenites, established the first Semitic hierarchy in Arabia's northern plateau. [3]

The concept of Black men being cursed also began in the East. Ogu Eji-Ofo Annu relates: "The original Black Arabs who were supposedly punished by destruction and deluge because, as legend has it in the book of Quran, they disobeyed their Prophets and flouted God's instructions; they were: Ad, Thamud, Tasam, Jadeis, and Imru. The classical Black Arabs, who are believed to have descended from Yaarub ibn Yashjub ibn Ghatan and thus called Ghataniyun. They had lived in the Yemen; they included a number of tribes and sub-tribes, two of which became historically prominent viz., Himyar and Kahlan (al'arab al'ariba). The Arabized Arabs: These tribes immigrated into Arabia from different sections of central Asia. Many of them intermarried with the desert dwelling nomadic blemmyes (nomadic Nubian tribe) - the Bejas (original Bedouin Arabs) and the Somali, Kenyan and Ethiopian tribes of Africa. Their mix-blood children who adopted a mingled form of their parent's cultures are known as the Arabized Arabs (al 'arab al musta 'riba)".[13]

The Arabized women seen above; namely, Miss Morocco, Miss Palestine, Miss Saudi Arabia, is not white but considered "red" according to the Arabic language. Al Dhahabi says "Red", in the speech of the people from the Hejaz (western Arabia), means fair-complexioned and this color is rare amongst the Arabs... **So it must be understood that what people call "white" today was called "red" by the Arabs of the past.**[14]

In addition to the hybrid influences made in the holy land (geographical pre-frontal cortex), we must mention the surrounding area of Jerusalem that is a combination between the geographical frontal lobe and prefrontal cortex as shown in illustration III.

*"Around the 13th century BC "sea people" around the northern Mediterranean Sea coasts vandalized coastal town and pirated ships. The Greek fleet suffered and Greek commerce in this sea degenerated which permitted the Phoenician City-States commerce and trade to prosper. Those "sea people", the ancient precursors of the "Vikings", spread havoc in Egypt before they were countered and then redeployed to Gaza [**Jerusalem**] and the*

Africoid
Cannanite God "El"

southern coast of Palestine (named after the sea people). It is plausible that the Palestinians returned not as a block but in waves to the Palestinian coasts. Many might have shipwrecked and many

---

[13] http://www.africaresource.com/rasta/sesostris-the-great-the-egyptian-hercules/the-original-black-african-arabs-of-arabia-part-1-ogu-eji-ofo-annu/

[14] http://www.africaresource.com/rasta/sesostris-the-great-the-egyptian-hercules/shades-of-arabic-skin-complexions-an-explanatory-note/

were lost in deserts before reaching the desert south region of Palestine.

"Moses and the nomadic "tribes" that he led out of the wilderness might be a symbolic tale or a mythical tale since there are no archeological facts or records in any civilization of the peregrination of these nomads up till they decided to settle down and seized towns by brute force. As these tribes got acquainted with Canaan civilization of the Land they set aside "Yahweh" for "El" the monolithic God of the Land. Now and then, a few of these nomad tribes generated "prophets" to remind them of "Yahweh" in period of dire disaster to strengthen tribal identity and pick up arms, devastation, and desolation. "Yahweh's" anger and thirst for revenge against civilized and settled people had no limits; the settled people had to suffer the raids of the desert nomads for loots and easy profits until the nomads learned to taste the fruits of civilized life.

*"The process of absorbing nomads into settled life was long; frequently new waves of nomads knocked on the doors of settled people in Canaan and Palestine. The new waves of nomads did not just emerge from the south but they also converged from the north (Turkey), the east (Persia), south-east (Arabic Peninsula), and the west (Greeks and sea people). **The Near East settled civilization, in City-States studded along the Euphrates, Tiger, Oronte Rivers and the coastal region, had to negotiate with warrior nations and infuse in these nations their monotheist religion and philosophy which spread all around the Middle East.** Like in every religion, every town and city had to adopt a patron saint or demi-god to consecrate and identify its particular characteristics or line of business. Thus, Baal, Astarte, Adonis, Apollo, and all the derivative demi-gods symbolizing the strength and bounty of nature were mere representations of particular aspects of the all powerful and omniscient God El."[15]*

Truth of the matter about Jerusalem is that **Jebus** (jē`bəs) or Jebusite (jĕb`yo͞osīt) in the Bible, **pre-Israelite tribes,** were the aboriginal founder[s] of Jerusalem. Then around 1300 BC more pale skin phenotype invaders from the Aegean Sea and Western Europe; appeared in mass numbers; began mixing with the pre-Israelite aboriginals until today hardly any reside in

---

[15] http://adonis49.wordpress.com/2009/07/12/the-sea-people-and-the-12-tribes/

Jerusalem except in the city of Jericho—one of the oldest continuously-inhabited cities in the world since to 9,000 BC.[16]

For the record, the original Black nation has been classified under many different appellations from pre-Israelites to primitives from pre-Adamites (pre-humans) to Negrito's. Modern historians pre-date Negrito's time on earth more than 100,000 years in the following global regions.

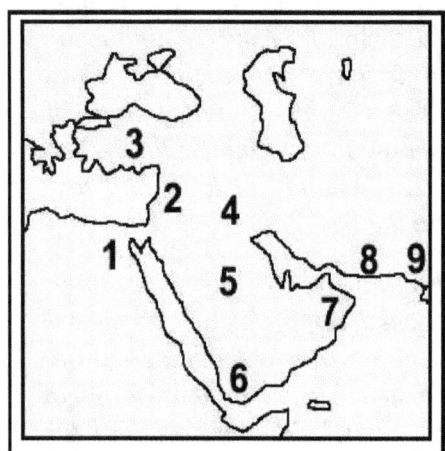

[Source:] The Palaeolithic of the Arabian Peninsula, *Journal of World Prehistory* 17:141-179, 2003.

Settlements of the Negrito-like people in the Near and Middle East.

1. Egypt
2. Lebanon, Israel, Syria
3. Turkey
4. Iraq, Kuwait
*5. **Arabia (Saudi Arabia)***
6. Yemen
7. Oman, Persian Gulf islands
8. Iran / 9. Pakistan: The Men of Makran (Gedrosians)

"The earliest migration of modern humans was likely to have taken place around 100,000 years ago and to have followed the coastlines.

"...around the Arabian Peninsula are not Negrids (modern black Africans) but are more likely to be Negritos or Veddoids. True, mere "looks" can be deceiving and do not provide a solid base for determining a population's ancestry. DNA analysis or craniometry would give much more reliable results. Unfortunately, the Negrito and Vedda-like people that interest us here are close to a taboo subject in the relevant countries. The Negrito are at the bottom of highly stratified, hierarchical societies and they tend to do the 'lowest' type of work, like rubbish collection. Even an expression of mild interest from an outsider in these people can cause sharply negative reactions which makes any kind of contact with (let alone providing help for or doing scientific research on) these unfortunate people practically impossible.[17]

---

[16] http://en.wikipedia.org/wiki/Jericho#Ancient_times
[17] http://www.andaman.org/BOOK/chapter47/text47.htm#arabia

The photographs capture such people taken by writer, explorer-anthropologist and photographer Carleton S. Coon.

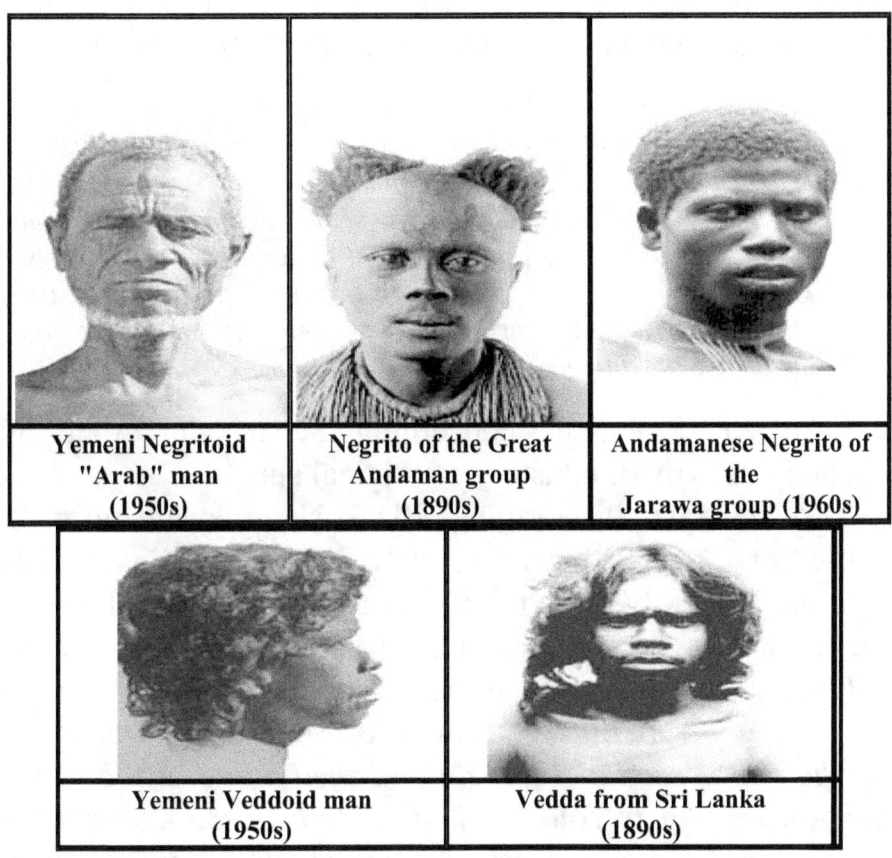

Yemeni Negritoid "Arab" man (1950s)	Negrito of the Great Andaman group (1890s)	Andamanese Negrito of the Jarawa group (1960s)
Yemeni Veddoid man (1950s)	**Vedda from Sri Lanka (1890s)**	

"...the Middle East has been inhabited since the dawn of history, we are led to suspect that some vestiges of ancient civilizations may have found their way into the caves of Arabia, nicely preserved and just waiting to be discovered. These speculations are somewhat supported by the discovery of various artifacts in Arabian caves during the last few years... Neolithic engraving in western Saudi Arabia may depict hunters using such  *missiles, suggesting that the throwing sticks could be (according to Dr. John Roobol) 6000-8000 BC..."*

The Bible speaks of how Adam and Eve committed their original sin in the East—Garden of Eden (Genesis 3). Ancient Arab legends speak of the original sin of a jinn race that rebelled in the Mecca 2,000 years before Adam i.e. 6000 years ago.

> *"Tradition tells us that Allah made the jinn two thousand years before He made Adam. Though invisible, they loved and married, begat children and died. In the beginning, all jinn were good, but long before the time of Adam they rebelled against their settled existence and tried to change the order of things. During the course of the revolt, one of the evil jinn, Iblis, gained great power and became the Satan of the Arab world. Iblis retained his power even after the angels of Allah had quelled the rebellion".* [18]

Ancient Egyptians concerning Sebau and Apep also predicted this symbolic history of original sin. [19]

At any rate, the Original Black Nation were ultimately crucified or removed from the seat of authority as stewards of the earth. The Holy Quran 2:30 verify how a new ruler would arise to replace the Original man (nation). *"Recall that your Lord said to the angels, "I am placing a representative (a temporary god) on Earth." They said, "Will You place therein one who will spread evil therein and shed blood, while we sing Your praises, glorify You, and uphold Your absolute authority?" He said, "I know what you do not know."* So as you can interpret, the root of this world's troubles began in the East—symbolic Garden of Eden.

The Honorable Elijah Muhammad taught that THE BLACK man has been ruling the earth for billions and trillions of years... and they have built many civilizations on this earth. Even where we are today (North America) once (long in the past) flourished with a fine civilization of the Black man who is the originator. This is what we mean when we say original or

---

[18] http://www.bible.ca/islam/library/islam-quotes-landau.htm

[19] Apep in ancient Egypt was a personification of darkness and Re had to fight him successfully every morning before he could rise from the east.

aboriginal. It means the first. I do think my people should be happy today to know that they are children of the first God.

The original God is our father, but not the father of the white man. The white man is made by an enemy of ours [Yacub or Jacob] who seized upon the chance to put an enemy to rule us into the opposite of our nature (righteousness). The only way he could get us to listen to such a made-man for 6,000 years was that he had to make him unalike. He had to make him with something to attract us.

SO OUR fathers of 6,000 years ago *(the original Black man of Arabia)* saw this unalike person emerging from the Island of the Aegean Sea and were attracted by this people—so much so—that they began to take them as friends and even to marry them and hide them away in their homes. They had been attracted by an unalike person. They had never seen a white human being before. He was not made in Arabia but he was made out of Arabia on an Island in the sea. He was not allowed to be made in the Holy Land. As the Bible teaches us, when Yacub's knowledge or idea of making the made-man was discovered they cast him and those who believed with him out (you will find this in Genesis) where it reads: *"Drive him out lest he put his hand on the tree of life and live forever."*[20]

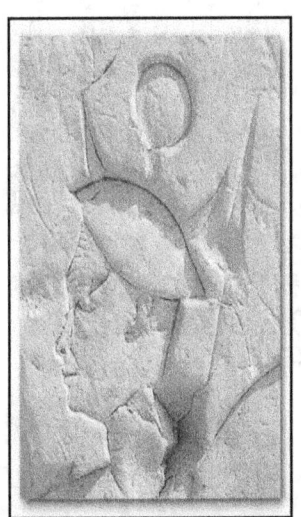

Images of the Sea People originating in the Aegean and Asia Minor as depicted in Ancient Egypt…"they began to enter Egypt, the warriors were usually accompanied by their wives and families, and it appears that they carried their possessions in ox-drawn cards, prepared to settle down though whatever territory they transverse". *Notice keen nose and thin lips. *Also compare image (r) headdress to image on pg. 33. **[Source]: http://touregypt.net/featuresto ries/seapeople]**

[20] http://www.muhammadspeaks.com/Unalikeattracts4-5-1968.html

The quintessence of the above history also explains where the "red" or Semitic people of Arabia originate *that is to say* interbreeding between the Original Black man and the primary Aegean Sea people who actually first entered the holy land 6,099 years ago from today. (See Chart A)

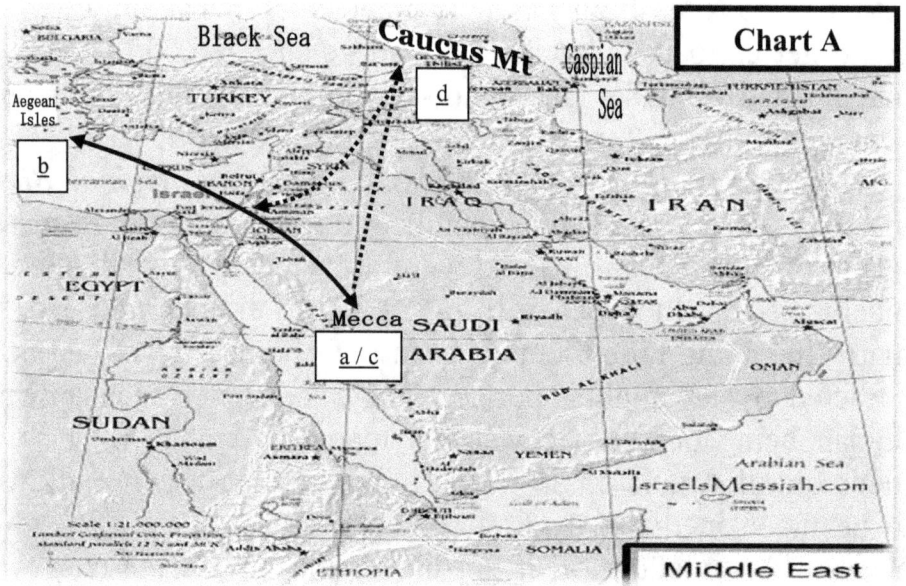

Of course, 6,000 years ago none of the present countries by name sake existed as shown in *chart A*. What you see; however, in steps *a*, *b*, *c* and *d* is a basic contour tracing the footsteps of Yacub's (Iblis[21]) rebellious original followers. They were first exiled from point **(a)** Mecca in year 8,400 (or 6,600 B.C.) to the Aegean Isles **(b)** or Patmos (Pelan) according the teachings of Elijah Muhammad. From here, 600 years later, in year 9,000 (4,000 B.C.), a pale skinned race returned to Mecca **(c)**. *(Some remained in the Mediterranean area on various Islands and near the coastlands thereof)*. But, upon arrival to Mecca, they generated trouble and were thus evicted into the

---

[21] **Apep was pictured as a serpent** or as a crocodile. There was a book written about Apep called *The Book of Overthrowing Apep and his fiends,* which gives spells and information on how to defeat him. These spells were recited daily in the temple of Amon-Re in Thebes.

Caucus Mountains—between the Black and Caspian Sea **(d)**, except for a small band. So how many were kept back in the holy land, enough to produce a Semitic stock. But the majority were evicted out of the holy land and exiled into the Caucus Mountains for 2,000 years where many lost all knowledge of institutional civilization thereby becoming completely savage until the coming of Mossa—their first prophet.

In 1933 the Honorable Elijah Muhammad responded to a lesson given to him by his Teacher. His answer is as follows:

"Mossa…taught him how to live a respectful life, how to build a home for himself and some of the Tricknollegy that Yacub taught him, which was devilishment - telling lies, stealing any how to master the original man. Mossa was a half-original, a prophet, which was predicted by the Twenty-Three Scientists in the Year One - fifteen thousand nineteen years ago today." **[Source: www.thenationofislam.org/lostfoundlesson.html]**

To more readily grasp a timeline or genesis of Yacub's epoch, review the calendar below.

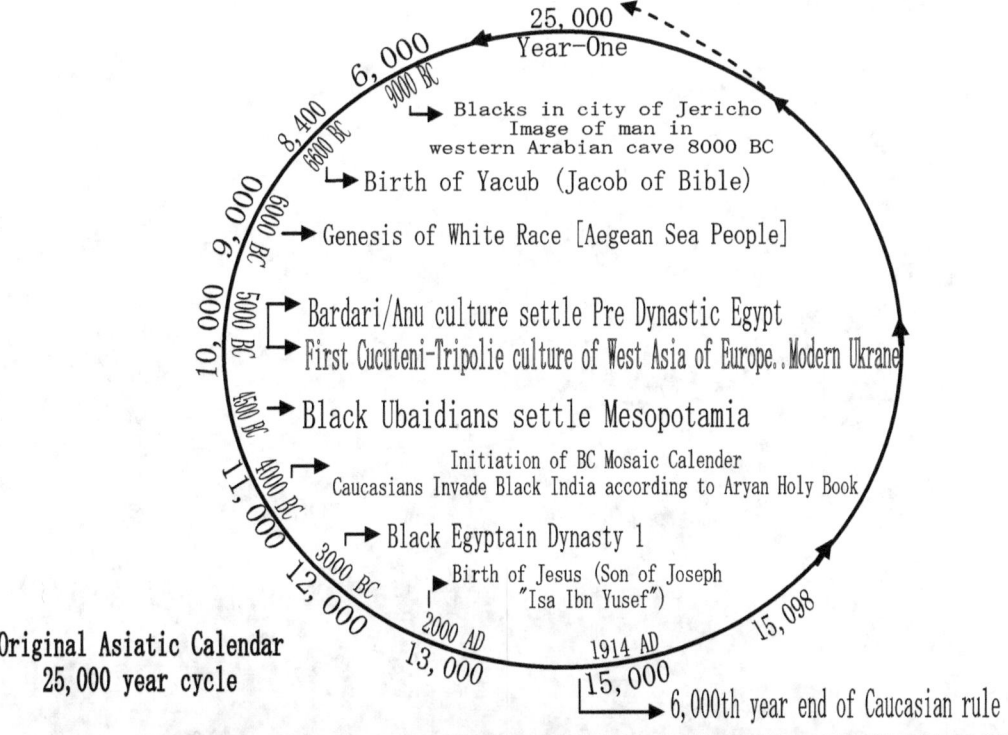

Original Asiatic Calendar
25,000 year cycle

Precession It takes to Earth's axis 25,771.5 years to make one full cycle before beginning a new cycle among the stars, centered on the ecliptic north pole with an angular radius of about 23.3°. [Source]: IAU 2006 Resolution B1, Adoption of the P03 Precession Theory and Definition of the Ecliptic)

I'll close this chapter offering one more body of research to demonstrate the purpose of the hidden history and mission of **CAUCASOIDS.**

"...today's genetic patterns...vividly reflect a historic event, or events, that occurred 3,000 or 4,000 years ago. The gene patterns 'are consistent with a historical scenario in which invading Caucasoids -- primarily males -- established the caste system and occupied the highest positions, placing the indigenous population, who were more similar to Asians, in lower caste positions.'

"The researchers, from the University of Utah and Andhra Pradesh University in India, used two sets of genes in their analyses...'Our expectations in this natural experiment are borne out when we look at the genes,' said Jorde. 'It's one of the few cases where we know the mating situation in a population for 150 generations. So it's kind of a test for how well the genes reflect a population's history. The ancient story holds that invaders known as Indo-Europeans, or true Aryans, came from Eastern Europe or western Asia and conquered the Indian subcontinent. The people they subdued descended from the original inhabitants who had arrived far earlier from Africa and from other parts of Asia."

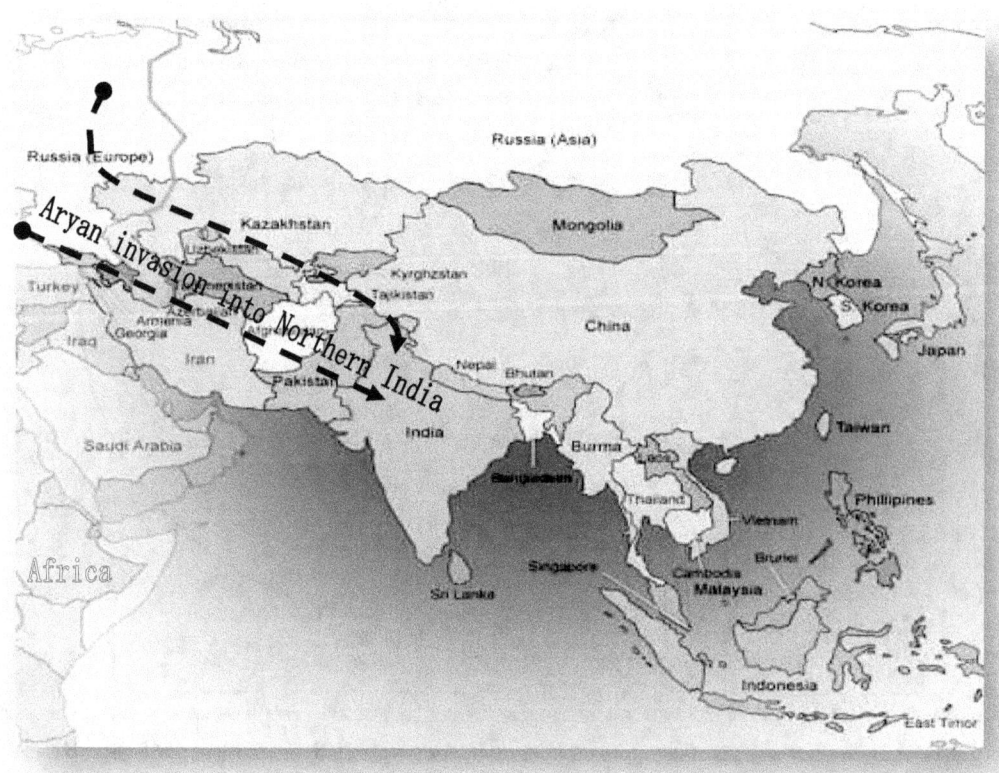

When Caucasians or "Aryans" invaded Northern India they seemed to have already held their own book of instructions called *"The Rig Veda"*. It was written in *Indo Aryan Sanskrit* containing a great many references to the race of the conquerors and the conquered. For example:

"According to the Rig Veda, the leader of the Aryan invasion was one Indra [God of War], and his role in 'slaying the Dasyus' (the Negroids in India) is prominent in the Rig Veda: 'Thou, Indra, art the destroyer of all the cities, **the slayer of the Dasyus,** *the prosperer of man, the lord of the sky.'*

" RgV. VIII 87.6 'The Rig Veda goes on to use the word 'black' in a number of instances to describe the Dasyu:

"The Rig Veda praises the god who **"destroyed the Dasyans and protected the Aryan colour."** *- Rg.V. III 34.9*

" RgV. IX 73 it is said that 'stormy gods who rush on like furious bulls and **scatter the black skin***',*

"...and it claims that 'the black skin, the hated of Indra' will be swept out of heaven - RgV. IX 73.5

"Rg.V. I 130.8 tells of how the 'black skin' was conquered: 'Indra protected in battle the Aryan worshipper, he subdued the lawless for Manu, **he conquered the black skin.***'*

"At the time of the writing of the main religious books of the Aryans - the Rigvedas - a distinction was drawn between the two types of people in the Indus river valley: the 'fair' conquering immigrants and the 'dark'  *native people. Within three hundred years however, physical mixing had proceeded to the point where these two racial classes had been subdivided further, with membership in each class being determined solely on the basis of how light or how dark an individual's skin color was. These divisions led to a color based class system being developed, known today as the caste system. The word caste was only given to the system by Portuguese travelers many centuries later, coming from the Latin word castus, meaning pure. The original Sanskrit for the caste system was 'varna', which means color. As assimilation and integration between the Aryans [whites] and the*

Dasyu [Blacks] increased, the caste system became more and more complex, till four major divisions were created, with membership in each group dependent upon the coloring of the individual. This four-tier system still exists in India today, with the highest caste, the Brahmans (or 'priests') being the lightest in color, and the Sudas or untouchables being the darkest.

"Within a few hundred years the original Aryans had become so assimilated that their contribution to Indian civilization can be considered to be at an end. Their legacy lives on in the language, religion and poetry of India - and of course the caste system.

The last of the Aryans can be found today in certain segments of Indian society, and most notably in that country's film industry, known as Bollywood.[22]

The argument here is that whether you call it Rigvedas, *Old Testament ideas*, apartheid, segregation, caste system or Willie Lynch theory, the Aryan invasion into Northern India represented how Yacub's grafted race successfully inserted themselves into a Divine lineage of the Original Black nation. As stated earlier by researchers from the University of Utah and Andhra Pradesh University in India, their invasion occurred between 4000 to 3000 years BC. Of course, this was two thousand years or more after their initial attempt to return to the East, Mecca Arabia.

In any event, the initial physiognomic (race mixing) with Northern India's Black population was experimental. It proved to Aryan (white race) how they could rule, in a roundabout way, over the Black nation through their offspring. And so, in this manner they are ruling directly yet indirectly over all original nation settlements except one, the Holy City Mecca, Arabia.

Of course, Mecca has its issues, but the mentality of the Caucasian race does not rule its inhabitants directly or indirectly. It remains in the hands of the descendants of the Original Black nation, directly, yet indirectly too!

---

[22] http://www.white-history.com/hwr5c.htm

CHAPTER 4

Black and White

The Bible Genesis contours the genesis of the people of Yacub (Jacob), but using its own symbolic terminology. It reads:

"After he had taken them (family) across the stream and had brought over all his possessions, Jacob was left there alone. Then some man wrestled with him until the break of dawn. When the man saw that he could not prevail over him, he struck Jacob's hip at its socket, so that the hip socket was wrenched as they wrestled. The man then said, "Let me go, for it is daybreak." But Jacob said, "I will not let you go until you bless me." "What is your name?" the man asked. He answered, "Jacob." Then the man said, "You shall no longer be spoken of as Jacob, but as Israel, because you have contended with divine and human beings and have prevailed." (Genesis 32:1-33)

Thus by force and rebellion, a new authority was posed to struggle into a status of power to rule over the first people of the earth. His name was Jacob whose grafted race was renamed Israel. Currently, the ruling monarch of this race represents the strength and wisdom of Caucasian intellect and ascendancy. In terms of their genetic makeup, they refer to themselves as carriers of the Kohanim gene (Y-chromosomal Haplogroup J1 (Y-DNA) since around 3,500 BC.

"Y-chromosomal Aaron *is the name given to the hypothesised most recent common ancestor of many of the patrilineal Jewish priestly caste known as Kohanim (singular "Kohen", "Cohen", or Kohane). In the Hebrew Bible this ancestor is identified as Aaron, the brother of Moses. Research published in 1997 and thereafter has indicated that some contemporary Jewish Kohanim share Y-chromosomal Haplogroup J1 (Y-DNA) with a set of genetic markers, known as the Cohen Modal Haplotype, which may well derive from a single common ancestor. Later, in 2007, the same team announced that they found another common set of genetic marker related to present-day* *traditional Kohanim families in Haplogroup J2 (Y-DNA).This J1 variant was called the **Cohen modal haplotype**."*[23]

The map below reveals how a particular people were settled in West Asia—Europe. After reviewing this map, review page 37 for more epoch clarification i.e. 25,000 years.

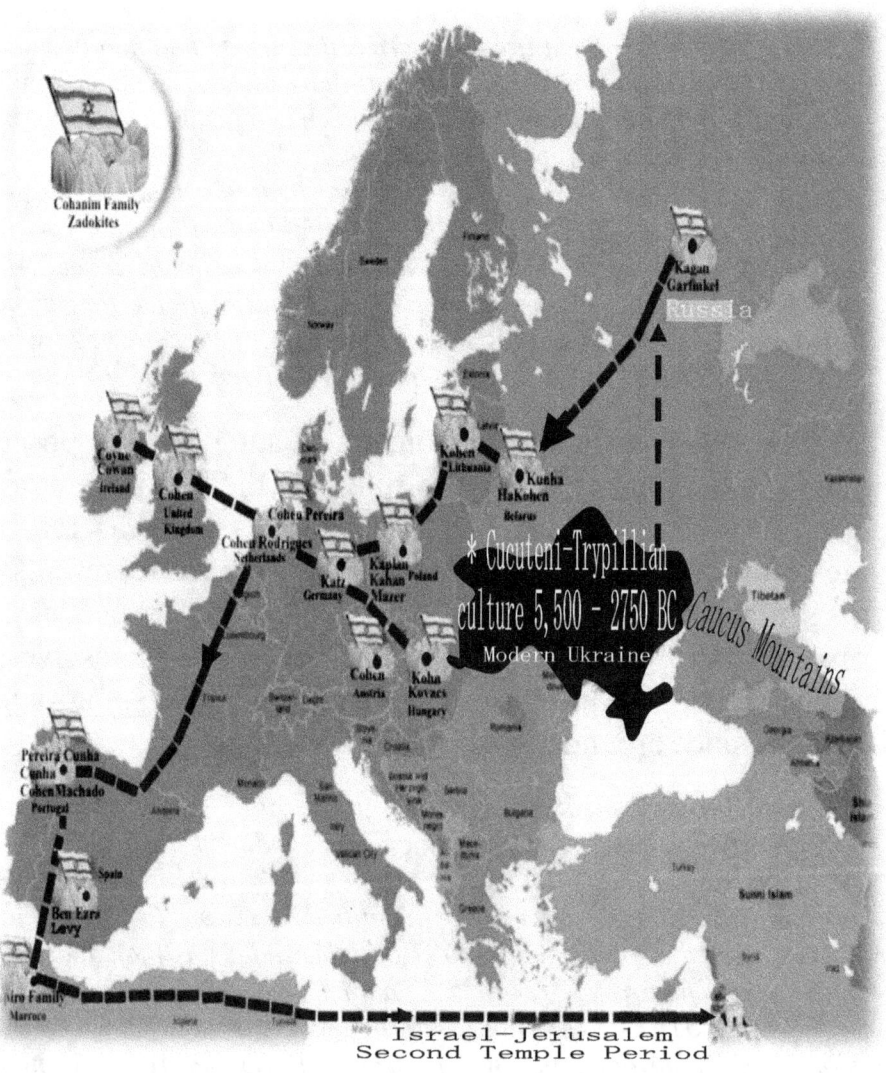

The above map partly shows how Joseph Felsenstein's scientific genetic computer software tracked the Kohanim (Cohen) gene, considering their haplotypes. Kohanim means

---

[23] http://en.wikipedia.org/wiki/Y-chromosomal_Aaron

priest or chaplain. This is because Cohanim Jews, Askenazi and Sephardi, for thousands of years preserved their genealogical lineages since the Temple period. They yet claim to have faithfully followed Cohanim Jewish tradition until this present day…

The Cohanim Tree places the correspondent families in the branches based on respective mutations. DNA results confirmed, by positioning the families in their respective places of origin, that the geographical location is correctly connected in genetics according to the Jewish tradition and records found in each one of these 21 different Cohanim families. It formed two branches, Ashkenazi and Sephardi. The Cohanim Sephardim is the older lineage compared to Cohanim Ashkenazim, though both of them are derived from the same common ancestor. The Shapiro family from Marrocos presented the oldest signature among all, passing from Sephardi branch in Spain, Portugal, and Netherlands and from there moving to Northern East Europe to Central and reaching Southern East Europe. As the history and records tells, correctly confirmed by DNA, Cohanim fled the Romans after destruction of the Temple and went to Marrocos, Spain/Portugal, to England, France, and Germany. In the 14th century many fled to Poland, Ukraine, Belarus, Lithuania, and Latvia."[24]

The wife of the Honorable Elijah Muhammad, Mother Tynetta Muhammad, summarized how some of Yacub's pale race avoided being exiled into the Caucus Mountains 6,000 years ago. She stated on June 12, 2009 in the Final Call Newspaper, *"A part of their race escaped by hiding out in some of the homes of the Original People in Arabia and ultimately made their way into the hills of what we call Central Asia or Eurasia and lived among the Original People in those parts of our planet. They did not go into the caves of Western Europe and took on the characteristics of the tribes living in that area of our planet. They were protected by the tribes in that entire area*

---

[24] http://en.wikipedia.org/wiki/Y-chromosomal_Aaron

all the way into the Caucasus Mountains in Russia where they co-mingled with the people there and are recognized in the history as the Sythians and other Nomadic Tribes that lived around the Black Sea and the Caspian Sea." (See map below of ancient Scythian territories)

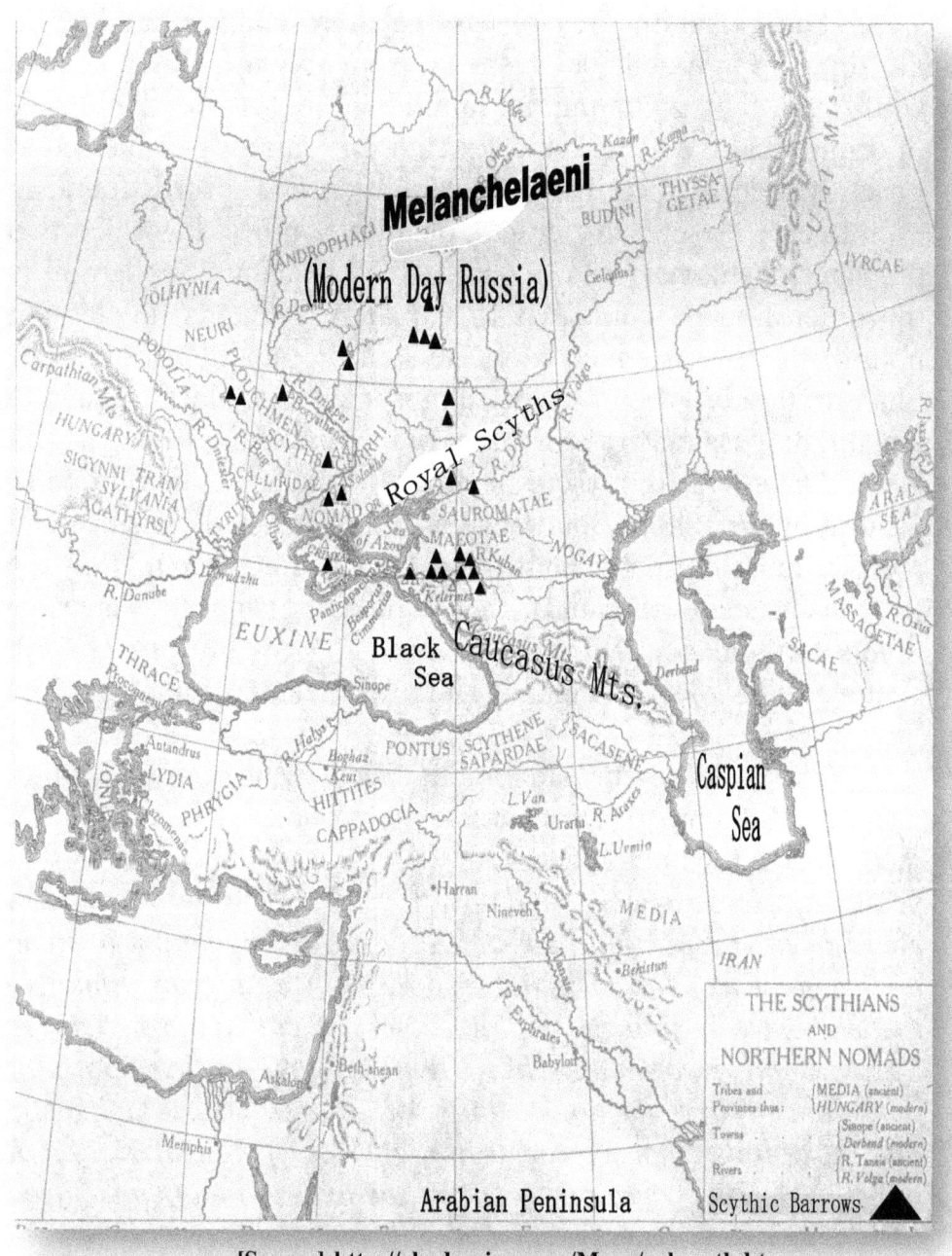

[Source]:http://rbedrosian.com/Maps/cahscyth.htm

*"On the opposite side of the Gerrhus is **the Royal district**, as it is called: here dwells the largest and bravest **of the Scythian tribes**, which **looks upon all the other tribes in the light of slaves**. Its country reaches on the south to Taurica, on the east to the trench dug by the sons of the blind slaves, the mart upon the Palus Maeotis, called Cremni (the Cliffs), and in part to the river Tanais. **North of the country** of the Royal Scythians **are the Melanchaeni (Black-Robes), a people of quite a different race from the Scythians**. Beyond them lie marshes and a region without inhabitants, so far as our knowledge reaches."[25]*

Scythian King

Around 450 BC the Greek historian Herodotus was able learn of the Scythians history and recorded what he learned. In *The History of Herodotus* by George Rawlinson, ed. and tr., vol. 3, Book 4, Chapters 2-36, 46-82. New York: D. Appleton and Company, 1885], we learn from Herodotus that Scythians believed themselves to have been the youngest of all nations. Although Herodotus did not believe their account, Scythians further stated to Herodotus that they were descendants of Targitaus, their first king—the offspring of the Egyptian Amun (whom Herodotus refers to as Zeus) and the daughter of a Scythian symbolically named Borysthenes.

This traditional Scythian history about *"Targitaus"* gives credence to what Elijah Muhammad revealed wherein he said:

"After 2,000 years of living as a savage, Allah raised up Musa (Moses) to bring the white race again into civilization: to take their place as rulers, as Yacub has intended for them. Musa (Moses) became their God and leader. He brought them out of the caves; taught them to believe in Allah; taught them to wear clothes; how to cook their food; how to season it with salt; what beef they should kill and eat; and, how to use fire for their service. Moses taught them against putting the female cow under burden. He established for them Friday as the day to eat fish, and not to eat meat (beef) on that day....

---

[25] http://www.shsu.edu/~his_ncp/Scythians.html

"...Moses taught the devils that if they would follow him and obey him, Allah would give them a place among the holy people. Most of them believed Moses, just to get out of the caves...The Imams recognized the tremendous job Musa (Moses) had, trying to civilize the savages. These enemies of the righteous black nation of earth now had to take the place as the rulers and conquerors of the earth. The devils were given the knowledge and power to bring every living thing, regardless of its kind of life, into subjection...

[Quote by Honorable Elijah Muhammad]

The name Scythian was assigned to them by the Greek historian Herodotus because he concentrated on the tribes living in modern Ukraine. They had the same name: in their own language, which belonged to the Indo-Iranian family, viz., *Skudat* ('archers'). The Persians rendered this name as *Sakâ* and the Greeks as *Skythai*. The Chinese called them, at a later stage in history, *Sai*. The oldest group we know of is usually called Indo-Iranian. (The old name *'Aryan'* is no longer used.) Around 1300 to 1400 BC they began invading the Middle East in mass to take the land of Canaan and Egypt from its aboriginal inhabitants. Much of this history was recorded on the Temple walls of the 18th and 19th Dynasties of Kemet (Egypt).

The invaders were descendants of Yacub's grafted race [Romans 11:17-24]. Such awareness was eventually made clear to the ancient rulers of all centers of Black civilization through their Priesthood, which answers archeological questions as to why the ancient centers of learning and religion were abandoned around in the organized sacred worlds' of South America, Asia, Africa, etc. Reason being, certain high-sciences were not to be taught to the early invaders—Sea people or "white race." Otherwise the Black nation would have never been able to rule again beyond the Caucasians silly mindset during end times or judgment day.

Sea People

The real ancient frescoes below depict aboriginal black, brown, red, yellow people living on the Aegean Islands with pale skin Sea People. From the research of these frescoes, it appears they were drawn before the great Aegean volcanic eruption around 1,628 B.C., which buried entire Islands throughout the Aegean Sea before Rome and Greece evolved as a power unto themselves.

Ancient Akrotiri,
Northeast Aegean

Carians
Patmos, Aegean Sea

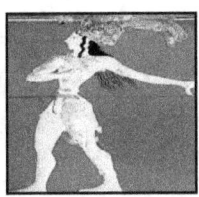

Palace of Knossos
Crete, Aegean Sea

Santorini
Southern Aegean Sea

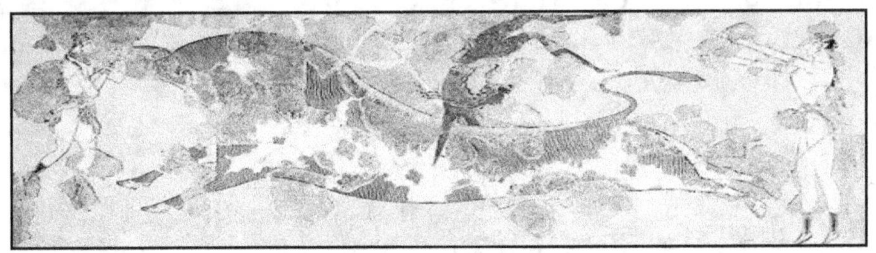

Fresco
Minion, Aegean Sea

Akrotiri Fresco
Northeast Aegean

Fresco
Minion, Aegean Sea

Boys boxing
Southwest Aegean

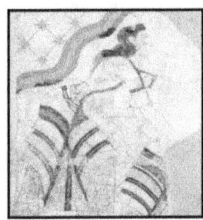

Santorini
Southern Aegean Sea

Modern Greeks shed light on the fact that a special branch of the white race—the Mediterranean branch—came from Asia and settled on the coast in the Aegean islands. They were called Aegean and their civilization was the Aegean civilization. However, the first inhabitants, they articulate, were pre Greeks and according to tradition, were known as Pelasgians referring to populations that preceded the <u>Hellenes</u> in <u>Greece</u>. Pelasgians is *"a hold-all term for any ancient, primitive and presumably autochthonous* (from Greek αύτόχθων "indigenous", from αύτο– + χθων "earth, soil".)[26] In other words, people of color—people of the earth—as seen in the ancient frescoes below.

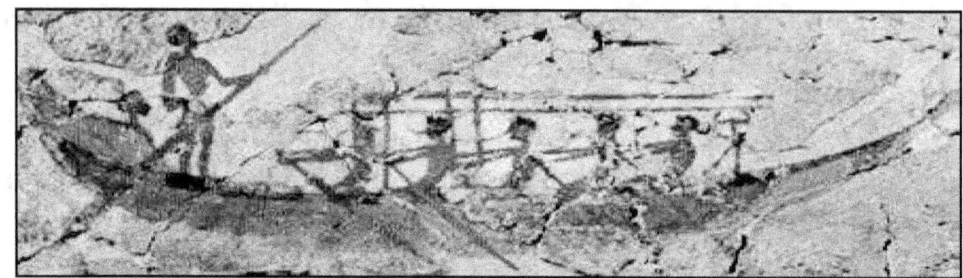

Fresco
A Pelasgian boat from Thera, Aegean Sea

So as the Honorable Elijah Muhammad said about what happened over Aegean Sea 6,600 years ago from today, i.e. it took 200 years to graft Black skin phenotypes to brownish-red and 200 years to graft Brownish-red to Yellow; and, lastly

Pelasgians

200 more years to graft yellow skin into a paleness. The porous between paleness, olive and tan are the reason modern Greeks acknowledge pre Greeks (Pelasgians). They detest acknowledging the more Black Pelasgians seen in the fresco of the boat from Thera, Aegean Sea.

Nevertheless, at the end of Yacub's experimentation, a de-melaninized[27] pale race emerged from the Aegean Sea Islands. De-melanized (recessive) is totally opposite of melanized (dominate) as the Bible Book of Romans {11:17-24} attempted to clarify:

*"**But if some of the branches were broken off** (Yacub and his 59,000 followers), **and you** (Caucasian race)**, although a wild olive shoot,***

---

[26] http://en.wikipedia.org/wiki/Autochthon

[27] In humans, melanin is the primary determinant of human skin color and also found in hair. The most common form of biological melanin is eumelanin, a brown-black polymer of dihydroxyindole, dihydroxyindole carboxylic acid, and their reduced forms.

were grafted in among the others (aboriginal body-politic) and now share in the nourishing root of the olive tree, do not be arrogant toward the branches. If you are, remember it is not you who support the root, but the root (Black nation) that supports you. Then you will say, "Branches were broken off so that I might be grafted in." That is true. They were broken off because of their unbelief, but you stand fast through faith. So do not become proud, but fear. For if God did not spare the natural branches (Original Black Nation), neither will he spare you (Caucasian race). Note then the kindness and the severity of God: severity toward those who have fallen (Original peoples lose of political prominence), but God's kindness to you, provided you continue in his kindness. Otherwise you too will be cut off (lose political prominence). And even they, if they do not continue in their unbelief, will be grafted in, for God has the power to graft them in again. For if you were cut from what is by nature a wild olive tree, and grafted, contrary to nature, into a cultivated olive tree, how much more will these, the natural branches, be grafted back into their own olive tree (Black nations will return to political prominence)."

The grafting process mentioned here was first a physical process performed by Yacub—the God of the Aegean Sea people or Caucasian race. A major attribute for their success as rulers ties to a theological importance meaning "chesed" "kindness" in Hebrew.

*"The word is used only in cases where there is some recognized tie between the parties concerned. It is not used indiscriminately of kindness in general, haphazard, kindly deeds; this is why Coverdale was careful to avoid using the word 'kindness' in respect of God's dealings with his people Israel. **The theological importance of the word chesed is that it stands more than any other word for the attitude which both parties to a covenant ought to maintain towards each other.**"* [28]

So as the ruling monarchs of the Caucasian race are yet attempting to maintain their political status in the holy land between the geographical frontal lobe and prefrontal cortex, their *covenant* is to remain united. (See maps on pages 26 and 36).

---

[28] http://www.bible-researcher.com/chesed.html

However, the irony is their unity does not connote good. It connotes a political relationship they were instructed to maintain between one another to rule over the original Black people of the earth until Allah see fits to complete "grafting" the Lost and Found mentality of North America into righteous Muslims.

A slow grinding process of unity between Black America and Africa will succeed as long as kindness *"for the attitude which both parties to a covenant ought to maintain towards each other"* is forged on all levels. After all, "chesed" (kindness) is what our ancient progenitors also desired for us, but after the 6,000-year rule of Yacub's people had their turn to rule. That time ended in 1914 AD.

What I want to clarify here is why so much kafuffle, war has and bloodshed occurred throughout Africa, the holy land and Eurasia over the past 6,000 years. Certainly *"official government"* scientists, scholars, researchers and men of religion have worked secretly to hide the truth about the original Black nation and the origin of the white race. Indeed a selected few have conspired to dismantle, disfigure, change color complexes, rewrite, misinterpret, halfway interpret, keep hush-hush the archeological digs and forensics of ancient aboriginal civilizations. The question is why! Simply put: envy and hatred.

Therefore, the contradictory forces of the ruling monarchs of the Caucasian race are laboring to prevent the Original nations' from legally reclaiming their land inheritance rights that were usurped centuries ago. Today Europe and America's ultra right wing entities continue their use of tricknollegy to maintain the promotion of a white God-ruled world, yet invisible God concept because they realize influencing minds is more valuable than paper money. Thus at all cost, the knowledge of the true and living God, Allah—the entire Black nation—must be barred from re-influencing the nations of the earth.

"The original man, Allah has declared, is none other than the black man. The black man is the first and the last, maker and owner of the universe. From him came all brown, yellow, red and white people. By

using a special method of birth control law the black man was able to produce the white race. The true nature of the Black and white mankind should be enough to awaken the so-call Negroes and put them on their feet and on the road to self-independence. Yet, they are so afraid of the slave-masters that they even love them to their destruction and wish that the bearer of truth would not tell the truth even if he knows it.

"The time has arrived when it must be told the world over. There are millions who do not know who is the original man. Why should this question be put before the world today? Because it is the time of judgment between the black and white and the knowledge of the rightful owners of the earth. Allah is now pointing out to the nations of earth their rightful places and this judgment will bring an end to war over it. Now it is so easy to recognize the original man, the real owner of the earth, by the history of the two (black and white). We have an unending past history of the black nation and a limited one of the white race.

"We find that history teaches that the earth was populated by the black nation ever since it was created, but the history of the white race does not take us beyond 6,000 years. Everywhere the white race has gone on our planet, they have either found the original man or a sign that he had been there previously. Allah is proving to the world of black men that the white race actually does not own any part of our planet.

"The Bible and the Holy Qur'an bears witness to the above, if you are able to understand it. The Holy Qur'an, the beauty of Scriptures, repeatedly challenges the white race to point out the part of the heavens and the earth that they created. It further teaches that they are not even their own creators. We created white man from a small life germ, the soft pronoun "we" used nearly throughout the Holy Qur'an makes the knowledge of the original man much clearer and more intelligent of how the white race's creation took place. In the Bible, referring to their creation, we have US (Gen. 1:26) creating, or rather making the race; the WE and WE used show beyond a shadow of a doubt that they came from another people.

"Knowledge of the white race removes once and for all times the mistakes that would be made in dealing with them. My followers and I can and are getting along with them in a more understandable way

51

than ever because we know them. You cannot blame one for the way he or she was born, for they had nothing to do with that. Can we say to them why don't you do the righteousness when nature did not give righteousness to them? Or say to them, why are you such a wicked devil? Who is responsible, the made or the maker? Yet we are not excused for following and practicing his evil or accepting him for a righteous guide just because he is not his maker.[29]

Elijah Muhammad Is Correct

Theologically speaking, a major aspect about the teachings of the Honorable Elijah Muhammad is inherent in the resurrection of an ancient theophany that ascribes God as a man (anthropomorphic) who would reveal the hidden mysteries after Yacub's rules of tricknollegy have ended. Furthermore, he went on to proclaim that the ancient Hebrew and Islamic prophecies concerning the coming of God in Person had indeed come true in the Personage of Wallace Fard Muhammad who revealed to him the hidden and astronomical mysteries of the ages. Of course, Eastern Muslim scholars and millions under their scholarship and tutelage vehemently rejected this teaching. But not so with the Western world, what they rejected of Elijah Muhammad was his teaching about the white race as a race of devils, which is why many classified him as a "hate teacher." Overall, Christian and Jewish scholars put forward little condemnation against Elijah Muhammad teaching Allah (God) is man.

> *"He, Mr. Yacub -- the mighty scientist and maker of the white race or white man was no fool by no means, just because he made and enemy for us. This made us still great to know that in us was the germ of a whole race of people -- that we could form him and teach him then make him to rule the teacher, for a certain length of time, until the people produced one greater than he (Yacub)...Now, today... "A Saviour is born"... out of the germ, out of the plunder..." He's made partly from the race of Yacub and partly from His own, just for the purpose to save you and me... "*[30]

---

[29] http://www.seventhfam.com/temple/books/black_man/blk29.htm
[30] http://www.muhammadspeaks.com/news.html

52

It turns out by all accounts, one Islamic scholar, Dr. Wesley Muhammad, actually evinces Allah (God) is a man and always has been according to Quranic language. According to his research the word Al-Ghaib, in particularly, in Quranic terminology describes the presence of Allah as a man or anthropomorphic being. Although most modern Islamic scholars say ghaib simply means "unseen" and attach its meaning as incorporeity (immateriality), Dr. Wesley Muhammad elaborates: "the word **'Al-Ghaib' means to 'withdraw ones presence from; absence from view' denoting 'a being that can be seen but has made a conscious decision to withdraw his presence until the appoint hour...'"**[31]

According to ancient Hebrew thought, YHWH also appears anthropomorphic. Some Old Testament writings seem to compel us to agree that the Coming of God as a man in the last days is authentic. *"I (YHWH) will raise them up a Prophet from among their brethren, like unto thee (Moses) and I will put my words in his mouth and he shall speak unto them all that I shall command him." (Deuteronomy 18:18)*

Francis Watson, of the University of Aberdeen points out: "YHWH appeared to Abraham at the oaks of Mamre" (Gen.18.1): like the previous chapter of Genesis, this one opens with a theophany, introduced in almost identical language (*wyera YHWH el Abram*, Gen.17.1; *wyera elyaw YHWH*, 18.1). On the earlier occasion, YHWH announced his own identity as *El Shadday*, and declared the terms of the covenant with Abram and his seed.

"Yet the two theophanies take a very different form. In the first one, the visual aspect is indeed assumed, for at its conclusion it is said that 'When he had finished talking with him, God went up from Abraham' (17.22). The speaker has been visibly present; Abraham does not simply hear a voice issuing as if from nowhere. And yet the visual aspect is completely subordinate to the auditory one. There is no concern to describe

---

[31] http://www.theblackgod.com/The%20Great%20Debate.pdf

what was seen, for all attention is focused on what was said. In the second theophany, however, what is seen is no less important than what is said and heard; indeed, what is seen appears to be in some tension with what is said and heard. Abraham seems aware from the start that this is indeed an appearance of YHWH (contrast Judges 13), but what he actually sees is not YHWH alone but 'three men standing in front of him' (Gen.18.2). Abraham 'ran to meet them' (liqr'atam), and his fulsome words of welcome are addressed initially to one only (v.3) but subsequently to the three (vv.4-5a); and it is the three that reply (wayomrw, v.5b)… The three eat together under the tree and call for Sarah, but it is YHWH who announces to Abraham that "your wife shall have a son" and who expresses his displeasure at Sarah's incredulity (vv.8-15). *[Journal For Scriptual Reasoning N0. 2.3 Sept. 2002]*

According to Dr. Wesley, Jesus of 2000 years ago evinced to the Jews that God is a man.

"16 Even if I do judge, my judgment is true, because I am not alone, but I and the Father who sent me. 17 And in your Law it is written that the testimony of two men (duo anthropon) is true. 18 I am the one who testifies about myself, and the Father who sent me also testifies about me."

"Jesus appeals to the Old Testament law governing the testimony of witnesses in order to support the validity of his own testimony. In referring to that law, however, he makes a significant change in the wording. The law reads, 'At the testimony of two witnesses (edim) ... a case shall be established (Deut. 19.15; cf. 17.6).' For the phrase 'two witnesses,' found in both the Hebrew and the Greek, Jesus substitutes 'two men.' In v. 18 he proceeds to apply this law to himself and his Father: he and the Father are the 'two Men' who testify. Thus as Jesus uses the phrase 'two Men' here, it paradoxically designates not two human beings, but two divine beings.

"In this passage Jesus does precisely the opposite of what one would expect. The natural expectation would be that if a law spoke of 'two men' and Jesus wanted to apply it to himself and God, he might change 'two men' to 'two witnesses' to avoid speaking of God as a man. In the present case, he could have simply retained the original wording of the law to avoid so speaking. Instead, he does the reverse. He apparently goes out of his way to apply the phrase 'two Men' to himself and god (emphasis added)." [32]

---

[32] http://www.finalcall.com/artman/publish/Columns_4/article_9572.shtml

CHAPTER 5

Father of the Caucasian Race

Wallace Fard Muhammad who was born 1877 in Mecca, Arabia, spiritually and mentally resurrected the Honorable Elijah Muhammad. FARD'S birth occurred 6,563 years after the death of the Yacub—the God of war.

The MASTER TEACHER taught the Honorable Elijah Muhammad that Yacub was the founder of unlike attracts and like repels, though Mr. Yacub was a member of the black nation. He began school at the age of four. He had an unusual sized head. When he had grown up, the others referred to him as the Big head scientist. At the age of 18 he had finished all of the colleges and universities of his nation, and was seen preaching on the streets of Mecca, making converts. He made such impressions on the people that many began following him. He learned from studying the germ of the black man, under the microscope, that there were two people in him, and that one was black, the other brown. He said if he could successfully separate the one from the other he could graft the brown germ into its last stage, which would be white. With his wisdom, he could make the white, which he discovered were the weaker of the black germ (which would be unalike) ruling the black nation for a time (until a greater one than Yacub was born).

This new idea put him to work finding the necessary converts to begin grafting his new race of people. He began by teaching Islam, with promises of luxury to those who would believe and follow him. As Mr. Yacub continued to preach for converts, he told his people that he would make the others work for them. (This promise came to pass).

Naturally, there are always some people around who would like to have others do their work. Those are the ones who feel for Mr. Yacub's teaching, 100 per cent. As he made converts in and around the Holy City of Mecca, persecutions set in. The authorities became afraid of such powerful teachings, with promises of luxury and making slaves of others. As they began making arrests of those who believed the teaching, the officers would go back and find, to their surprise, others still teaching and believing it. Finally they arrested Mr. Yacub. But, it only increased the teachings. They kept persecuting and arresting Yacub's followers until they filled all the jails. The officers finally reported to the King that there was no room to put a prisoner in -- if arrested. All the jails are filled; and, when we go out into the streets, we find them still teaching. What shall we do with them? The King questioned the officers on just what the teachings were; and of the name of the leader. The officers gave the King the answers to everything. The King said: This is not the name of that man.

On entering the prison, the King was shown Yacub's cell. Wa-Alaikum. The King said: So you are Mr. Yacub? He said: Yes, I am. The King said: Yacub, I have come to see if we could work out some agreement that would bring about an end to this trouble. What would you suggest? Mr. Yacub told the King: If you give me and my followers everything to start civilization as you have, and furnish us with money and other necessities of life for twenty years, I will take my followers and we will go from you. The King was pleased with the suggestion or condition made by Yacub, and agreed to take care of them for twenty years, until Yacub's followers were able to go for themselves. After learning who Mr. Yacub was, they all were afraid of him, and were glad to make almost any agreement with him and his followers.

This history or future of Mr. Yacub and his people was in the Nation's Book, by the writers (23 Scientists) of our history… before his birth. So, the Government began to make preparation for the exiling of Mr. Yacub and his followers. The King ordered everyone rounded up who was a believer in Mr. Yacub. They took them to the seaport and loaded them on ships. After rounding them all up into ships, they numbered 59,999. Yacub made 60,000.

Their ships sailed out to an Isle in the Aegean Sea called Pelan (Bible Patmos). After they were loaded into the ships, Mr. Yacub examined each of them to see if they were 100 per cent with him; and to see if they were all healthy and productive people. If not, he would throw them off. Some were found to be unfit and overboard they went. When they arrived at the Isle, Mr. Yacub said to them: See how they (the Holy people) have cast us out. Now -- if you will choose me to be your King, I will teach you how to go back and rule them all. Of course, they had already chosen Yacub to be their King at the very start. So, Yacub chose doctors, ministers, nurses and a cremator for his top laborers. He called these laborers together and told them his plan for making a new people, who would rule for 6,000 years.

He called the doctor first and said: Doctor, let all the people come to you who want to marry; and if there come to you two real black ones, take a needle and get a little of their blood and go into your room and pretend to be examining it, to see whether their blood would mix. Then, come and tell them that they will each have to find another mate, because their blood does not mix. (It was the aim of Yacub to get rid of the black and he did.) Give them a certificate to take to the minister, warning the minister against marrying the couple because their blood does not mix. When there comes to you two browner ones, take a pretended blood test of them; but, give them a certificate saying that they are eligible to marry.

Mr. Yacub's charge to his laborers was very strict -- death if one disobeyed. They didn't know what Yacub had in mind until they were given their labor to do. He made his laborers, from the chief to the least, liars. The doctor lied about the blood of the two black people who wanted to marry, that it did not mix. The brown and black could not be married (brown only)... After the first 200 years, Mr. Yacub had done away with the black babies, and all were brown. After another 200 years, he had all yellow or red, which was 400 years after being on Pelan. Another 200 years, which brings us to the six hundredth year, Mr. Yacub had an all-pale white race of people on this Isle.

Of course, Mr. Yacub lived but 150 years but his ideas continued in practice. He gave his people guidance in the form of literature. What they should do and how to do it (how to rule the black nation). He said to them: When you become unalike (white), you may return to the Holy Land and people, from whom you were exiled…There was no good taught to them while on the Island. By teaching the nurses to kill the black baby and save the brown baby, so as to graft the white out of it; by lying to the black mother of the baby, this lie was born into the very nature of the white baby; and, murder for the black people also born in them -- or made by nature a liar and murderer…This is what Jesus learned to their history, before He gave up His work of trying to convert the Jews or white race to the religion of Islam. And, the same knowledge of them was given to Muhammad [of Arabia] by the Imams (or scientists) of Mecca. That is why the war of the Muslims against them came to a stop. Muhammad was told that he could not reform the devils and that the race had 1,400 more years to live; [after the death of Muhammad] the only way to make righteous people (Muslims) out of them was to graft them back into the black nation.

This grieved Muhammad so much that it caused him heart trouble until his death (age sixty-two and one half years). The old scientists used to laugh at Muhammad for thinking that he could convert them (the devils) to Islam. This hurt his heart.

Mr. Yacub taught his made devils on Pelan: That -- when you go back to the holy black nation, rent a room in their homes. Teach your wives to go out the next morning around the neighbors of the people, and tell that you heard her talking about them last night. When you have gotten them fighting and killing each other, then ask them to let you help settle their disputes, and restore peace among them. If they agree, then you will be able to rule them both. This method the white race practices on the black nation, the world over. They upset their peace by putting one against the other, and then rule them after dividing them.

This is the reason why the American so-called Negroes can never agree on unity among themselves, which would put them on top overnight. The devils keep them divided by paid informers from among themselves. They keep such fools among us. But, the real truth of the devils sometimes converts the informers and brings them over to us as true believers. We don't bother about killing them, as I am not teaching that which I want to be kept as a secret, but that which the world has not known and should know.

After Yacub's devils were among the Holy people of Islam (the black nation) for six months, they had our people at war with each other. The holy people were unable to understand, just why they could not get along in peace with each other, until they took the matter to the King.

The King told the holy people of the black nation that the trouble they were having was caused by the white devils in their midst, and that there would be no peace among them until they drove these white made devils from among them. The holy people prepared to drive the devils out from among them. The King said: Gather every one of the devils up and strip them of our costume. Put an apron on them to hide their nakedness. Take all literature from them and take them by way of the desert. Send a caravan, armed with rifles, to keep the devils going westward. Don't allow one of them to turn back; and, if they are lucky enough to get across the Arabian Desert, let them go into the hills of West Asia, the place they now call Europe.

Yacub's made devils were driven out of Paradise, into the hills of West Asia (Europe), and stripped of everything but the language. They walked across that hot, sandy desert, into the land where long years of both trouble and joy awaited them; but -- they finally made it. (Not all: many died in the desert.) Once there, they were roped in, to keep them out of Paradise. To make sure, the Muslims, who lived along the borders of East and West Asia, were ordered to patrol the border to keep Yacub's devils in West Asia (now called Europe), so that the original nation of black man could live in peace; and the devils could be alone to themselves, to do as they pleased, as long as they didn't try crossing the East border. The soldiers patrolled the **border**[33] armed with swords, to prevent the devils from crossing. This went on for 2,000 years. After that time, Musa (Moses) was born: the man whom Allah would send to these exiled devils to bring them again into the light of civilization. Before we take up this first 2,000 years of the devils exiled on our planet, let us not lose sight of what and how they were made, and of the god who made them, Mr. Yacub.

Since we have learned that Mr. Yacub was an original man (black) the ignorant of our people may say: If Yacub was a black man and the father of the devils, then he was a devil. That is like one saying the horse is as much a mule as the mule. Or, that an orange or lemon is as much grapefruit as the grapefruit: because the grapefruit is grafted from the orange and lemon. They are not alike because the grafted is no longer original.

Just what have we learned, or rather are learning from this divine revelation of our enemies, the devils? Answer: We are learning the truth, which has been kept a secret for 6,000 years concerning the white race, who have deceived us. We learn what is meant by the Bible's symbolic teachings: that they were made from dust. This only tends to convey the idea that they were created from nothing; which means the low and humble origin of such creation. Again, we learn who the Bible (Genesis 1:16) is referring to in the saying: Let us make man. This US was fifty-nine thousand, nine hundred and ninety-nine (59,999) black men and women; making or grafting them into the likeness or image

---

[33] The border represents **East Turkey**, its main sights where religious centers, cities and underground fortresses were built 6,000 – 10,000 BC. *[http://www.ancient-wisdom.co.uk/turkey.htm]*

of the original man. Now that they are the same, but have the ways of a human being they are referred to as mankind -- not the real original man, but a being made like the original in the sense of human beings.

The Holy Quran throws a great light on the truth of the creation of this pale, white race of devils. O mankind, surely we have created you from a male and a female (Chap. 49:15). This makes it very easy to understand to whom it is referring. What mankind? Surely we created man from sperm mixed (with ovum) to try him, so we have made him hearing and seeing (Chap. 76:2). Inasmuch as these chapters have a further reference to the spiritual creation of the Last Messenger, it is equally true that they refer to the physical creation of the white race. In another place, the Holy Quran says: We have created man, and now he is an open disputer.

Yacub's race of devils was exiled into the hills and caves of West Asia (now called Europe). They were without anything to start civilization and became savages. They remained in such condition for 2,000 years--no guide or literature. They lost all knowledge of civilization. The Lord, God of Islam, taught me that some of them tried to graft themselves back into the black nation, but they had nothing to go by. A few were lucky enough to make a start, and got as far as what you call the gorilla. In fact, all of the monkey family is from this 2,000 year history of the white race in Europe. Being deprived of divine guidance for their disobedience, the making of mischief and causing bloodshed in the holy nation of the original black people by lies, they became so savage that they lost all their sense of shame. They started going nude as they are doing today (and leading the so-called Negroes into the very acts). They became shameless. In the winter they wore animal skins for clothes and grew hair all over their bodies and faces like all the other wild animals. In those days, they made their homes in the caves on hillsides.

There is a whole chapter devoted to them in the Holy Quran-an. They had it very hard, trying to save themselves from being destroyed by wild beasts, which were plentiful at that time in Europe. Being without a guide, they started walking on their hands and feet like all animals; and, learned to climb trees as well as any of the animals. At night, they would climb up into trees, carrying large stones and clubs, to fight the wild beasts that would come prowling around at night, to keep them from eating their families. Their next and best weapons were the dogs. They tamed some of these dogs to live in the caves with their families, to help protect them from the wild beasts. After a time, the dog held a high place among the family because of his fearlessness to attack the enemies of his master. Today, the dog is still loved by the white race and is given more justice than the so-called Negroes, and, is called the white man's best friend. This comes from the cave days.

After 2,000 years of living as a savage, Allah raised up Musa (Moses) to bring the white race again into civilization: to take their place as rulers, as Yacub has intended for them. Musa (Moses) became their God and leader. He brought them out of the caves; taught them to believe in Allah; taught them to wear clothes; how to cook their food; how to season it with salt; what beef they should kill and eat; and, how to use fire for their service. Moses taught them against putting the female cow under burden. He established for them Friday as the day to eat fish, and not to eat meat (beef) on that day. And, fish is the main menu on Fridays in many of the whites' homes today.

They were so cvil (savage) that Moses had to build a ring of fire around him at night; and, he would sleep in the center of the ring to keep the devils from harming him. They were afraid of fire, and are still afraid of fire. Allah said that: One day, Moses told them he was going to have fish come up from the sea that so that tomorrow we will have some fish. On the next day, the fish were there. Moses had a boatload sent up from Egypt. Moses said: See! The sea came up last night and brought us some fish. One of the savages was a little smart and he said to Moses: Where is the water? From then on, Moses recognized the fact that he could not say just anything to them. He had a hard time trying to civilize them. Once they gave Moses so much trouble that he took a few sticks of dynamite, went up on the mountainside, placed them into the group, and went back to get those who were giving him the most trouble. He said to them: Stand there on the edge of this mountain and you will hear the voice of God. They stood there about 300 in number. Moses set the fuse off and it killed all of them.

The Imams got after Moses for performing this trick on the devils. Moses said to the Imams: If you only knew how much trouble these devils give me, you would do as I do. Moses taught the devils that if they would follow him and obey him, Allah would give them a place among the holy people. Most of them believed Moses, just to get out of the caves.

The Imams recognized the tremendous job Musa (Moses) had, trying to civilize the savages. These enemies of the righteous black nation of earth now had to take the place as the rulers and conquerors of the earth. The devils were given the knowledge and power to bring every living thing, regardless of its kind of life, into subjection. And God said: *"Let us make man in our image, after our likeness: Let them have dominion over the fish of the sea; and over the fowl of the air; and over the cattle, and over all the earth; and over every creeping thing that creepeth upon the earth: and God said unto them: Be fruitful and multiply; and replenish the earth, and subdue it."* (Gen. 1:26, 28) The above was all necessary if the devils were to rule as a God of the world. They must conquer, and bring into subjection, all life upon the earth -- not land life alone, but they must subdue the sea and the like therein -- master everything, until a greater master of God comes, which would mean the end of their power over the life of our earth.

We all bear witness that the scripture quoted above refers to the Caucasian race. They are the only people who answer that description and word for the past 4,000 years. They have subdued the people and most every kind of living thing upon the earth. God has blessed them to exercise all their knowledge, and blessed them with guides (prophets) from among our own people; and, with the rain and seasons of the earth. Today, their wealth is great upon the earth. Their sciences of worldly good have sent them, not only after the wealth of other than their own people, but even after the lives and property of their own kind. They have tired to re-people (replenish) the earth with their own kind, by skillfully killing off the black man and mixing their blood into the black woman. But, the job is too big for them to ever conquer. The black nation including its other three colors, brown, red and yellow, outnumber the Caucasian race, eleven to one. God created them in His image (Gen. 1:27). They are in the image and likeness of a human being (black man), but is altogether different kind of human being than that of the black human beings…[34]

With the above said, year 2013 will be 6,699 years from the grafting of Yacub's race—Jacob meaning *usurper* or *deceiver*—who God later renamed as Israel.[35] When they and Yacub's followers were evicted from the Holy Land, the following Quranic historiography was fulfilled, *"Get you down (upon the earth), all of you together, from Paradise, some of you are an enemy to some others. Then, if there comes to you guidance from Me, whoever follows My Guidance shall neither go astray, nor fall into distress and misery."* (Quran 20:123)

Dominant and Recessive Genes

For scientific evidence to demonstrate the white or pale skin race were produced over 6,000 years ago from original black people, you must appreciate the scientific formula **genotype + environment + random-variation = phenotype.** I also suggest you read what was exposed in Philadelphia, Pennsylvania—at the American Association of Physical Anthropologists meeting,—a new report on the evolution of a

---

[34] http://www.muhammadspeaks.com/Makingofdevil.html
[35] http://www.keyway.ca/htm2000/20001101.htm

gene for skin color that suggested Europeans acquired pale skin quite recently, perhaps only **6000** to 12,000 **years ago**. Yes in 2005, researchers linked the paleness of the modern European skin to a **mutation in gene SLC 24A5**. Its implication is immense if fully comprehended. The "whites" or Caucasians are not native to Europe as noted by Sokal. Haak et al (2006) [36]

Gathered from the research of these European genetic scientists and others, it only proves that Black man and women (progenitors to us all) were the first humans of creation from which all races derived not to exclude the "red" Arabs, "white" Christians and European Jews.

*"O mankind! We created you **from** a single (pair) of a male and a female, and made you into nations and tribes, that ye may know each other (not that ye may despise (each other). Verily the most honoured of you in the sight of God is (he who is) the most righteous of you. And God has full knowledge and is well acquainted with all things."(Holy Quran 49:13)*

To quote the Honorable Elijah Muhammad once again, he said the Quranic verse *"Surely I am going to **create a mortal of the essence of black mud** fashioned in shape"* *(Holy Quran Sharrieff, 15:28)* means "the essence of the black nation which actually means the sperm of the black nation..." The question becomes: What did Yacub see in the essence of his nation? In part he saw the inner works of the *"incomplete dominant gene"* or melanin in two types: <u>pheomelanin</u> *(yellow to red-brown)* and <u>eumelanin</u> *(brown to black)*. Both amount and type is

---

[36] http://www.sciencemag.org/cgi/content/short/316/5823/364a

determined by (4) to (6) genes which operate under <u>incomplete</u> <u>dominance</u>."[37]

Essentially *"incomplete dominance"* represents that the recessive gene [*a*] is hidden within the dominant gene [*A*]. By this design, it is shown as [*Aa*]. Through experimentation viz., the 6 determinant genes in <u>eumelanin</u>, Yacub was able to determine how to make a [*aa*] genetically recessive race of people. Prior to his concept, there were no recessive [*aa*] phenotypes in civilization with disagreeable characteristics promoting chaos and disorder by nature. The Original nation was either genetically <u>pheomelanin</u> or <u>eumelanin</u> that is, [*Aa*] incomplete dominance or [*AA*] dominance by the Creator of the Universe. As crude as it might seem, the white race were made under the number 6 (sex) and the sperm of the Black nation was used to genetically graft them over 6,000 years ago.

"...Yacub discovered in the germ of the Black man that a brown germ was there also. And he made a white person through grafting from the brown germ. This made the made-man unalike from the self-created man (the Black man). "The Black man is self-created, while white mankind is a made-man by experimenting with the germs and ideas of the maker. The idea of the maker was to make one to rule the original Black man (who is self-created and has no birth record of his creation). He had to make him an unalike man of the original man. Therefore, he grafted his made-man unalike. He knew the science of unalike attracts while alike repels..."Their scientists know this because we have our mark on them. They couldn't deny it if they tried. If they know how to go into it...."

"...IN OUR 25-thousand-year cycle of making history for our Nation, there was a vacuum of 6,000 years. This Yacub, the father of the white man, was aware of. Therefore, he put his made-man in the vacuum to rule. This vacuum extended from the 9,000th year to the 15,000th year of our calendar history, so God (in the Person of Master Fard Muhammad) to whom praises are due forever, taught me. His making the made-man unalike to attract alike was a perfect job. He foresaw the end of the unalike made-man, and was perfect in knowledge that this type man could rule alike (the original man). Therefore, Mr. Yacub's idea became a fruitful one. He would make a man an enemy to his original self and kind, (Yacub was an

---

[37] http://en.wikipedia.org/wiki/Pale_%28skin_tone%29#Melanin_and_genes

original man.) This made-man's wisdom had no permanence and would be limited to the coming of an alike person to take over his way of rule.[38]

What you have just read is the physical making of Adam as mentioned in Bible Genesis and Quran. Not the spiritual exegesis or Preadamite history. Between 1968-73 when the Honorable Elijah Muhammad spoke the above words *"we have our mark on them...if they know how to go into it"* he was actually alluding to what modern geneticist call ***"genetic markers"***. These markers are specific and produce a readily recognizable genetic trait that can be used in family and population studies or in linkage analysis. Otherwise known as a Haplogroup, which means the study of genetic molecular evolution. For instance:

"Y-chromosomal Adam is the name given by researchers to the male who is the most recent common patrilineal (male-lineage) ancestor of all living humans. Major Y-chromosome haplogroups, and their geographical regions of occurrence (prior to the recent European colonization), include:

Groups without mutation M168

Haplogroup A (M91) Africa, especially the Khoisan, Ethiopians, and Nilotes *[Sudan]*.

Haplogroup B (M60) Africa, especially the Pygmies and Hadzabe.

 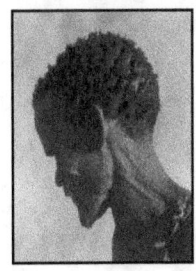

---

[38] http:// www.muhammadspeaks.com/Unalikeattracts4-5-1968.html

Groups with mutation M168

Haplogroup C (M130) Oceania, North/Central/East Asia, North America and significant presence in India. *__Haplogroup D__* (M174) Tibet, Japan, the Andaman Islands. *__Haplogroup E1b1a__* (M2) Africa); formerly known as E3a. *__Haplogroup E1b1b__* (M35) East Africa "Ethiopians and Somalis", North Africa "Berbers and Arabs", the Middle East, the Mediterranean, the Balkans; formerly known as E3b peoples in <u>Dagestan</u>; J1 with DYS388=13 is associated with eastern Anatolia."[39]

Modern geneticists have recently discovered that all other races throughout to entire planet are descendants of **Haloplo A** and **Haloplo B**. Furthermore, genetic researchers and scientists have admitted that all other Haplogroups after A & B are subgroups with mutations, yet contain some identifiable genetic marker related to the Original Black nation in some form, shape or fashion.

The view more details into the scientific making of the white race, order *"Black People White People: Who Is the Devil"* by Rasheed L. Muhammad.

---

[39] http://genealogy.wikia.com/wiki/Human_Y-chromosome_DNA_haplogroups

CHAPTER 6

Ancient Egypt

The brain is the fundamental core of the nervous system and is by far the most intricate, complicated and powerful part of the human body. It is responsible for both the lower order functions (such as digesting and breathing) and the higher order functions (such as thinking and inventing). It is at the root of most characteristics that set us apart from simpler forms of animals (language, rationality, mathematics, etc.) All sectors of the brain perform some function, and many of them will be performed in parallel.

This book presents Egypt arbitrarily on the geographical brain maps primary motor cortex area, a region containing large neurons known as Betz cells, which send long axons down the spinal cord to synapse onto alpha motor neurons, which connect to the muscles. All neuroscience confirms if someone's motor cortex is destroyed by a stroke, for example, he or she loses the ability to [plan and execute refined movements or] make precise movements, especially of the hands and fingers.[40] (See Illustration IV)

In more ways than one, no intelligent person will argue about the brilliant building accomplishments made by the hands of Ancient Egyptians. Alas, these ancient hands no longer build anything for themselves. Therefore, I ask, what damage has occurred to the brain of their offspring that hinders them from nationhood building?

---

[40] http://thebrain.mcgill.ca/flash/i/i_06/i_06_cr/i_06_cr_mou/i_06_cr_mou.html

Exhibits (a) of statues above depict the strength of ancient black men who once ruled over ancient Egypt. Statues of these Nubian kings up to ten feet high were found buried at the Nubian capital of Kerma, in Sudan. Smashed during Egyptian King Psamtek II's incursion south around 593 B.C., they were recently reassembled.[41] Next, notice exhibit (b): the "back pack" and "purse" carried and worn by ancient Egyptian women. Lastly, in exhibit (c) we have *Egyptian-Nubian* Queen Tye.

Illustration IV

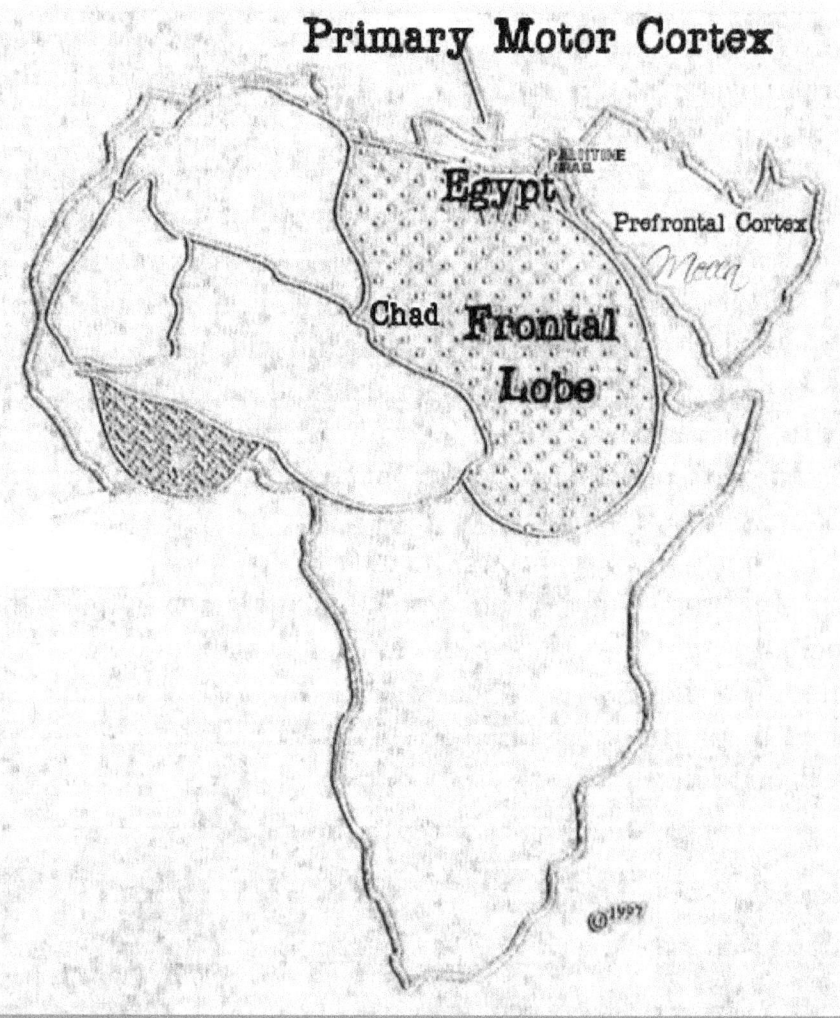

[41] http://ngm.nationalgeographic.com/2008/02/black-pharaohs/ken-garrett-photography.html

The most famous works known to mankind are the three great pyramids at Giza, the Sphinx and the prophetic writings of the ancient Egyptian Priesthood. Sadly, there are those in Hollywood who have attempted to demonize ancient Egypt's intelligence to hide the truth about her brilliance and contributions to humanity. Professor Cheikh Anta Diop, however, decoded the name by which "Egyptians" defined themselves i.e., *kmtjwthe* [hieroglyphics] meaning "black men".

In 1830, Howard Vyse, an English astronomer became convinced that the Pyramid in its design and construction evidenced a wonderful knowledge of astronomy, applied mathematically and other scientific information, predating our recorded knowledge by several thousand years. Mr. Robert Menzies of Leith Scotland is given credit for being the first to attract general attention to the assertion that the Great Pyramid was treasury of divinely given wisdom embodying chronological, meteorological, astronomical, mathematical, historical and biblical truth. He also contented that this storehouse of wisdom remained sealed by Divine appointment, to be revealed to those now living; to which these truths would bear witness, at a time they would be most needed. [4]

To your right is a Pre Dynastic Black man of Egypt. This "Tera-neter" tile was found by British Egyptologist W.M. Flinders Petrie in 1853 at the early temple at Abydos underneath the dynastic temple. This proto-historic figure of *Tera-neter*, a nobleman of the Anu or Aunu race is considered some the  first inhabitants of Pre Dynastic Egypt around 5500 B.C. (Review page 37 for timeline clarification)

"Egyptologist, Professor William Flinders Petrie in his book 'The Making of Egypt', 1939 wrote that the first king of Egypt [Menes] had a strong Negro face with characteristic features which dominated that period. In reality, the other Pharaohs of the dynasty were no less Negroid; Petrie affirmed...'that this dynasty, the first to give Egyptian civilization its almost definitive form and expression, was of

Sudanese Nubian origin. The equally Negro's features of the protodynastic face of <u>Tera Neter</u> and those of the first king to unify the valley, also prove that this is the only valid hypothesis. Similarly, the Negro's features of the Fourth Dynasty Pharaohs, the builders of the great pyramids, confirm this." Petrie the founder of pre-dynastic Nile Valley archaeology, excavated at Nagada and Ballas in Upper Egypt nearly 100 years ago, un-earth nearly 1200 pre-dynastic graves. It was Petrie's conviction that there was "a peaceful", if not a united, rule all over Egypt and Nubia [Sudan] during the entire pre-dynastic period. It was Petrie's conviction that there was "a peaceful", if not a united, rule all over Egypt and Nubia [Sudan] during the entire pre-dynastic period." [42]

Basically ancient *"Anu"* Egyptians designed and organized the most elaborate and complex system of education ever known to any civilization. During their rule they laid the foundation for all highly civilized nations of the globe long before any foreign sociopath, and invader had entered its borders. Ancient Egypt was so highly developed that before its decline the bible read: *"Now after they had left, an angel of the Lord appeared to Joseph in a dream and said, "Get up, take the child and his mother, and flee to Egypt, and remain there until I tell you; for Herod is about to search for the child, to destroy him." Then Joseph got up, took the child and his mother by night, and went to Egypt, and remained there until the death of Herod. This was to fulfill what had been spoken by the Lord through the prophet, "Out of Egypt I have called my son."* (Matthew 2:13-15) Isn't this fascinating! The Lord said, take "the child and his mother, and flee to Egypt". Of course Egypt was once considered, land of the Black Gods.

*"The ancient **Egyptians** were a Hamitic people and even though they have been in some way involved with the origin of the Ishmaelite Arabs, they remained a distinguishable people that have not been assimilated by the Arab invaders. The Egyptians became Christians in the first centuries c.e., and their genuine descendants are the Copts, who are not Arabs. Even though at present they are a minority*

---

[42] http://wysinger.homestead.com/proof.html

in their own homeland, the Arab majority is anyway the result of a foreign invasion performed in the Middle Ages, when the Arabs made of Egypt the outpost for the conquest of Africa."[43]

The key operative words above are *foreign invasion.* Such invasions began because, in part, the Aegean Sea people were instructed to perpetuate an evil that would pass through the land of the original nations' of the globe for a season and for a reason.

"4. And the foolish among us used to forge extravagant lies against Allah: 5. And we thought that men and jinn did no utter a lie against Allah: 6. And persons from among men used to seek refuge with persons from among the jinn, so they increased them in evil doing: 7. And they thought, as you think, that Allah would not raise anyone: 8. And we sought to reach heaven, but we found it filled with strong guards and flames: 9. And we used to sit in some of the sitting- places thereof to steal a hearing. But he who tries to listen now finds a flame lying in wait for him: 10. And some of us are good and others of us are below that----we are sects following different ways. 11. And we know that we cannot escape Allah in the earth, nor can we escape Him by flight: 12. And when we heard the guidance, we believed in it. So whoever believes in his Lord, he fears neither loss nor injustice: 13. And some of us are those who submit, and some of us are deviators. So whoever submits, these are at the right way. 14. And as to deviators, they are fuel of hell:" (Quran 72:4-14)

The Honorable Elijah Muhammad said of the above, "you have the verses of Truth in Chapter 72 of the Holy Quran. These verses are so plain that they do not need any interpretation, because these things have now come to pass. Foreign Believers here mean white believers; not other than white. The chapter is headed under the name "Jinn" here means the devil. **Verse 4** is a warning to you who are by nature created a Muslim, my Black People of America' who seek refuge among the devils. The devils deny your coming to them and believing as they believe against Allah. The **5th verse** teaches us, in using the words men

---

43 http://www.imninalu.net/myths-Arabs.htm

and jinn, that this is meaning the Black Man and the devil. Jinn are the devil and men are the Black People. Those who profess that they are teaching scripture of the Bible and the Holy Quran think ignorant thoughts; that the devil does not lie in what he says of the Bible and Holy Quran, and that this is true. The average Black Man thinks that every word of the Bible is the Truth. But, this is their belief on the surface and not underneath the surface where we get the knowledge of what is said or written of scripture. But, it all should be understood. LOOK HOW the average preacher of Christianity boasts that the Bible and all that he preaches and that which he adds of imaginary understanding or explanations is Truth. But, it is not truth: and he does not know the real Truth of the Bible. The **6th verse** teaches us that the devil only increases you in evil doings. The **7th verse** reveals the disbelievers in the Resurrection of the mentally dead Black People of America. The 8th verse refers to the devil as trying to reach outer space, as they are now doing. The heavens here mean the planets, which have life on them. As you know, they are trying to learn of the life that is on Venus and Mars through instruments. They would like to make pictures of the Martians and of the life on Venus. They have learned that what Allah has revealed to me is the Truth as they now have learned, today; from the knowledge of the moon. THAT WHICH Allah has taught me, and what I have written in this paper and in other news items for thirty years or more is the Truth. They found the moon to be as Allah taught me and they are afraid to put foot on that soil unless they are well cased in with oxygen of this Earth; for they will die almost instantly if they are not well shielded and protected from moon's magnetic power. The moon has no water on it. While we are born on the Earth, out of water. Therefore, it takes an environment that has water for us to exist and breathe that kind of atmosphere. We see the **8th verse** of this chapter now being fulfilled. The white man is doing all that was predicted that he would do, and he should not do other than that lest the prophecy of it in the Book would be considered a lie, But, we cannot call the God and His Prophets liars and get away with it, because they speak the Truth. THEY SEEK to reach the heavens (planets) to see what they hold (what is on them) and the devil confesses in the eighth verse, that they found the heavens filled with strong guards and flames. This is also mentioned in the Holy Quran in another place where Allah Says He put strong guards in the Heavens. It is protected: well protected. And the Bible promises that if they did go up to heaven, they would be brought back down to hell. So, these things must be fulfilled. We are right in the fulfillment of the prophecy where the devil is trying to get up into the planets atmosphere to get a peep: to see exactly what the nature of the life on the surface of these planets are like. But, before he can do these things, he will be stopped. He is not meant to know and to contact the life on these planets by throwing flames of fire at them (meteors) for if they are allowed to get to the life of other planets, especially Mars and Venus, they would probably try to interfere with that peaceful life. Especially Mars, which has a true life.

ALLAH (GOD) taught me that the Original Black Man has pictures of the people on Mars and even has extracted their language and now understands how to communicate with them in their own language. This, the white man would like to learn if this is true or not, by his exploration of space and the planets. I am sorry. Mr. White Man, these are secrets that you are not permitted to learn. You may be able to send a camera over the planets but I advise you to stay away from them. The **9th verse** teaches us that the devil does sit in on the Muslims and seeks to learn what is going on among the Muslims, as he has already confessed. He keeps his mechanical car on the Muslims to see what is going on: and this is what he wants to do in his space travels. He is seeking to learn what is happening on other planets, but a flame of fire is set and is lying in wait for him…"[44]

---

[44] http://www.muhammadspeaks.com/JinnForeignBel.html

Poor Black nation invaded and overrun by the Jinn race and now believe in a mystery God. But only for a season and for a divine reason.

Ancient Chad

As we continue to examine the Mother Continent, let us review Chad. Due to its distance from the sea and its largely desert climate, Chad is sometimes referred to as the *"Dead Heart of Africa"*. Cave paintings; nonetheless, indicate Chad was once a fertile and populous country in ancient times.

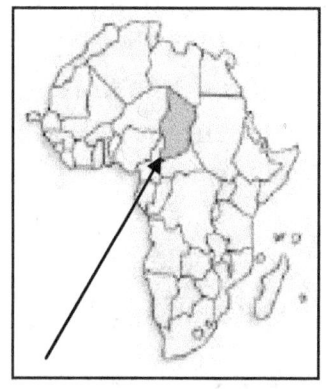

By the 9th century AD, the kingdom of Kanem was established in what is now western Chad, with its capital at Njimi, near Mao. Kanem-Bornu Empire, in the Lake Chad region, lasted for a thousand years, from the 9th to the 19th century. It was founded by the Kanuri, a mixed negroid and Berber people living east of Lake Chad, and was ruled by *mais*, or kings, of the Saifawa dynasty. Based on trans-Saharan trade, the state was early subject to the influences of Islam, which in the 11th century became the accepted religion.

Conquests during the next 200 years expanded the empire as far west as the Niger River and east to Wadai; to the north its power extended into the Fezzan. In the 14th century, wars with the Bulala people to the south forced the *mai* to move west to Bornu, where succeeding *mais* reestablished the empire and, under Ali Ghaji, founded a new capital at Ngazargamu. The 16th century was one of renewed expansion and power, especially under Idris Alooma, who had acquired firearms from North African Turks. The empire declined again in the 18th century, due in part to infiltration by the Fulani from the west. Barely withstanding an onslaught by Usuman dan Fodio in 1808-9, the empire was finally absorbed by Wadai in 1846.[45]

What we can deduce thus far about the Black nation of ancient Chad is that war was on its mind too. But what was their objective? They like all others; before and after them were attempting to MAKE A RULER, gain control of trade and commerce and direct the orthodox of the mind of the people to whom would serve under what is deemed a centralized government system!

Chad is fixed on the pre-motor cortex of the geographical brain map. (See Illustration V)

The primary motor cortex (Egypt), as shown in Illustration IV, works in association with the pre-motor cortex (Chad). The pre-motor cortex helps to guide skeletal body movements by integrating sensory information, and it controls the muscles that are closest to the body's main axis. It is also involved in planning actions (in concert with the basal ganglia)

---

[45] http://encarta.msn.com/encyclopedia_761562065_4/Chad.html

and refining movements based upon sensory input, this of course requires the cerebellum.[46]

Illustration V

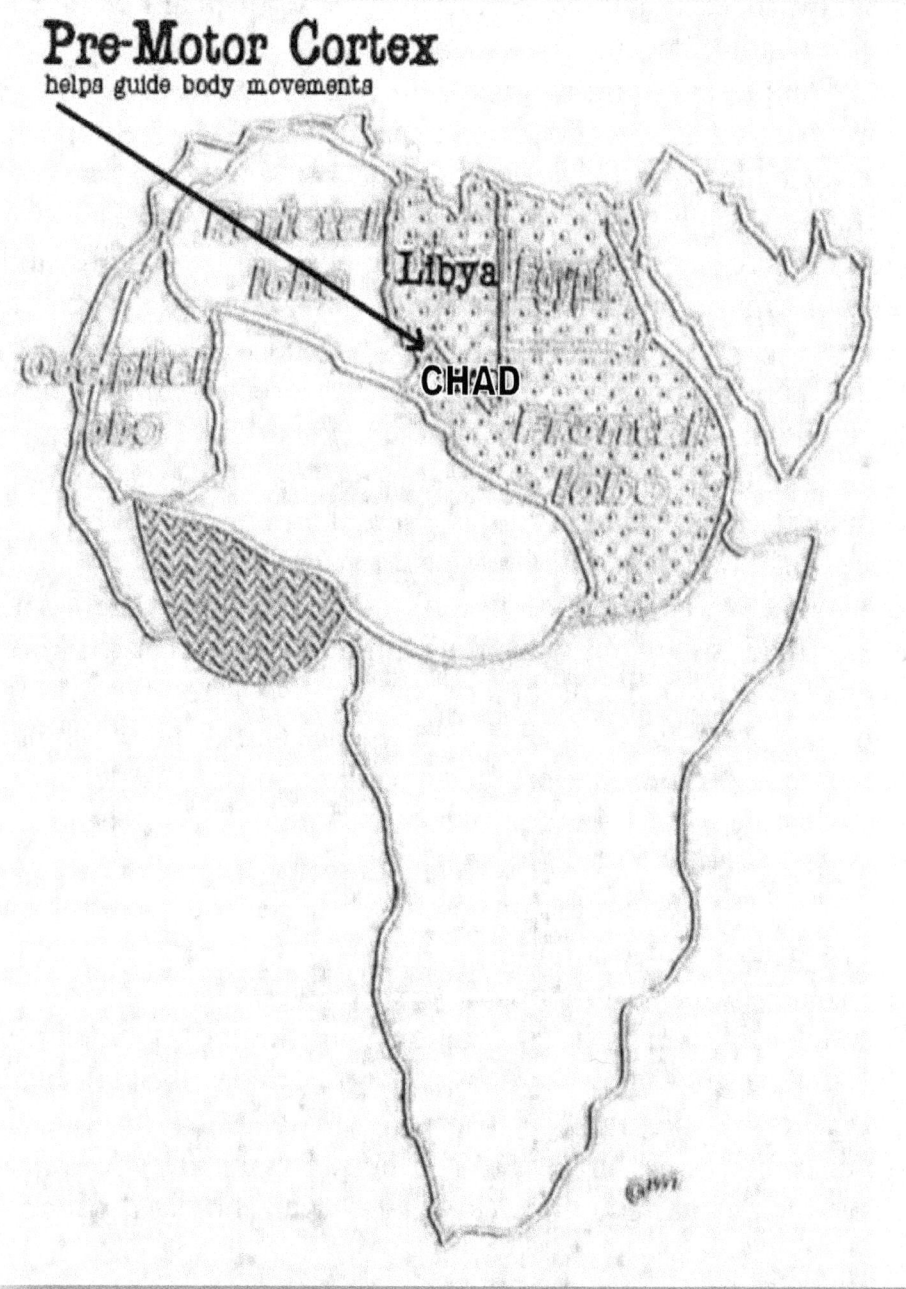

[46] http://en.wikipeia.org/wiki/Primary_mo

CHAPTER 7

Yoruba Tribe of Africa

So far I have attempted to subjectively demonstrate how Mother Africa, her Original inhabitants and the brain are connected in more ways than one. Fact is Africa and the history of the holy land is so old that much of it has been shrouded in mythological tradition, legend, and metaphor. Yet at its base is the truth. The Honorable Elijah Muhammad has revealed such truths.

In 1962 he lectured that an ancient tribe viz., Shabazz was in Africa dating back 50,000 years. And other tribes or families has been produced since that time and has spread out over the Earth. He said don't make a mistake in thinking that this was the beginning of the man on the Earth. Fifty thousand years ago is like telling you thirty days ago or ten days ago or five days ago, to the age of the universe. We have no exact record of it but it runs way into the trillions. Shabazz was the tribe that originally founded the ancient city of Mecca (Bakkah) after moon and earth split apart 66 trillion years ago.

"...Islam was the religion of the black people who lived before Adam was made, as far back as 66 trillion years ago when the earth and the moon were together and formed one and the same planet . . . and which at that time was called 'moon' instead of earth. (Not really by the word 'moon' that we use today, but by a word in Arabic that means practically the same thing.)" **[Elijah Muhammad (Vol. 1, No. 4) Muhammad Speaks Newspaper]**

Quranic history reveals Mecca (whose more ancient name is Bakkah) is where the first house of worship (Kaaba) appointed for mankind was established. The Kaaba is Islam's most sacred sanctuary and pilgrimage shrine. According to the Quran, the cubic-shaped Kaaba was built by Adam according to a divine plan and rebuilt by Abraham and Ishmael. When Prophet Mohammed began to preach to the Meccans, the Kaaba was a shrine for the pagan deities of the Arabs. After the Prophet established control of Mecca, the shrine was rededicated to Allah in 631 AD.

All Muslims face toward the Kaaba during their daily prayers. Mecca (Bakkah) is also addressed as **Umm ul-Qurâ** i.e., Mother of the Settlements (towns). *"The most important shrine established for the people is the one in __Becca__; a blessed beacon for all the people. In it are clear signs: the station of Abraham. Anyone who enters it shall be granted safe passage. The people owe it to GOD that they shall observe Hajj to this shrine, when they can afford it. As for those who disbelieve, GOD does not need anyone." [Quran; 3:96-97]*

The Bible Psalms also mentions a valley named __*Baca*__ in connection with the pilgrimage (Islamic Hajj). Below is a quote from Psalms 84:1-6:

> *"How lovely is your dwelling place, O LORD Almighty! My soul yearns, even faints, for the courts of the LORD; my heart and my flesh cry out for the living God. Even the sparrow has found a home, and the swallow a nest for herself, where she may have her young-- a place near your altar, O LORD Almighty, my King and my God. Blessed are those who dwell in your house; they are ever praising you. Blessed are those whose strength is in you, who have set their hearts on pilgrimage. As they pass through the __Valley of Baca__, they make it a place of springs; the autumn rains also cover it with pools."*

As you can read from the Bible Palmists description of ancient Bakkah (Baca), he was reminiscing about a time when it was fertile territory, yet a place where pilgrimage was in place during *pre-Islamic* times. Generally speaking; however, the whole of Arabia is the homeland of Original Black men and women whom modern day Arabs refer to as very Adam.[47]

---

[47] **The Arabs used the "shadeed al udma (very adam)".** When the Arabs described another Arab as black-skinned, they were only expressing the fact that the person was so dark-skinned that he/she was black. (source: http://savethetruearabs.com/gpage2.html)

Ali A. Mazuri, author of The Africans: A Triple Heritage may have also given credence to teachings of Mr. Muhammad as well. He says on page 300 of his book, "Another major African group whose origins have been traced to the other side of the Red Sea are the Yoruba, now mainly concentrated in Nigeria and Benin. One legend has it that Yoruba are the remnant of the children of Canaan, who were of the 'tribe of Nimrod'. The cause of their establishment in the West of Africa was…in consequence of their being driven by Yorraooba, son of Kastan, out of Arabia to the Western coast between Egypt and Abyssinia. From that spot, they advanced into the interior of Africa until they reached Yarba, where they fixed their residence.

According to a related mythological tradition, 'the Yoruba migrated from Mecca to present abode, having been forced out of Mecca following a civil war involving Oduduwa, son of King Lamurudu of Mecca. Oduduwa became the common ancestor of the Yoruba as a Black African people, and Ile-Ife was the place from which Yoruba culture flowered in West Africa…"[5]

Yoruba King Terracota

Yoruba Women

Whether you accept what Ali Muzuri writes or what Mr. Elijah Muhammad revealed, before its fall West Africans indeed fulfilled a magnificent function in their areas' of the [g]lobe.

"It was gold from the great empires of West Africa, Ghana, Mali and Songhay, which provided the means for the economic take off of Europe in the 13th and 14th centuries and aroused the interest of Europeans in western Africa. An early historian in the 9th century wrote 'the king of Ghana is a great king. In his territory are mines of gold.' When the famous historian of Muslim Spain, al-Bakri wrote

about Ghana in the 11th century, he reported that its king 'rules an enormous kingdom and has great power'. The king of Ghana was said to have an army of 200,000 men and to rule over an extremely wealthy trading empire. In the 14th century, the West African Empire of Mali was larger than Western Europe and reputed to be one of the largest, richest and most powerful states in the world. The Moroccan traveler Ibn Batuta wrote about his very favorable impressions of this empire and said that he found 'complete and general safety' there. "[48]

To make one more analysis about West Africa's cerebellum and the countries around its region; namely; Nigeria, Liberia, Sierra Leone, Togo, Benin, Burkina Faso, Côte d'Ivoire, Guinea, Guinea-Bissau and Ghana you must review the following neurological terms.

1. **_Cerebellum_**--*sometimes referred to as the "little brain," the cerebellum lies on top of the pons, behind the brain stem. The cerebellum is comprised of small lobes and receives information from the balance system of the inner ear, sensory nerves, and the auditory and visual systems. It is involved in the coordination of motor movements as well as basic facets of memory and learning.*

2. **_Midbrain and Pons_**--*The midbrain controls many important functions such as the visual and auditory systems as well as eye movement. Portions of the midbrain called the red nucleus and the substantia nigra are involved in the control of body movement. The pons relays sensory information between the cerebellum and cerebrum; aids in relaying other messages in the brain; controls arousal, and regulates respiration (see respiratory centres). In some theories, the pons has a role in dreaming.*

With anticipation, use your own perception to devise some insight into these neurological terms that may add more light to understanding the function of Nigeria, Liberia, Sierra Leone, Togo, Benin, Burkina Faso, Côte d'Ivoire, Guinea, Guinea-Bissau and Ghana and their peoples' relationship with humanity that I have attempted to parallel thus far. (See Illustration VI)

---

[48] www.antislavery.org/breakingthesilence/main/briefings/1.%20Africa%20before%20the%20Transatlantic%20Slave%20Trade.doc

Illustration VI

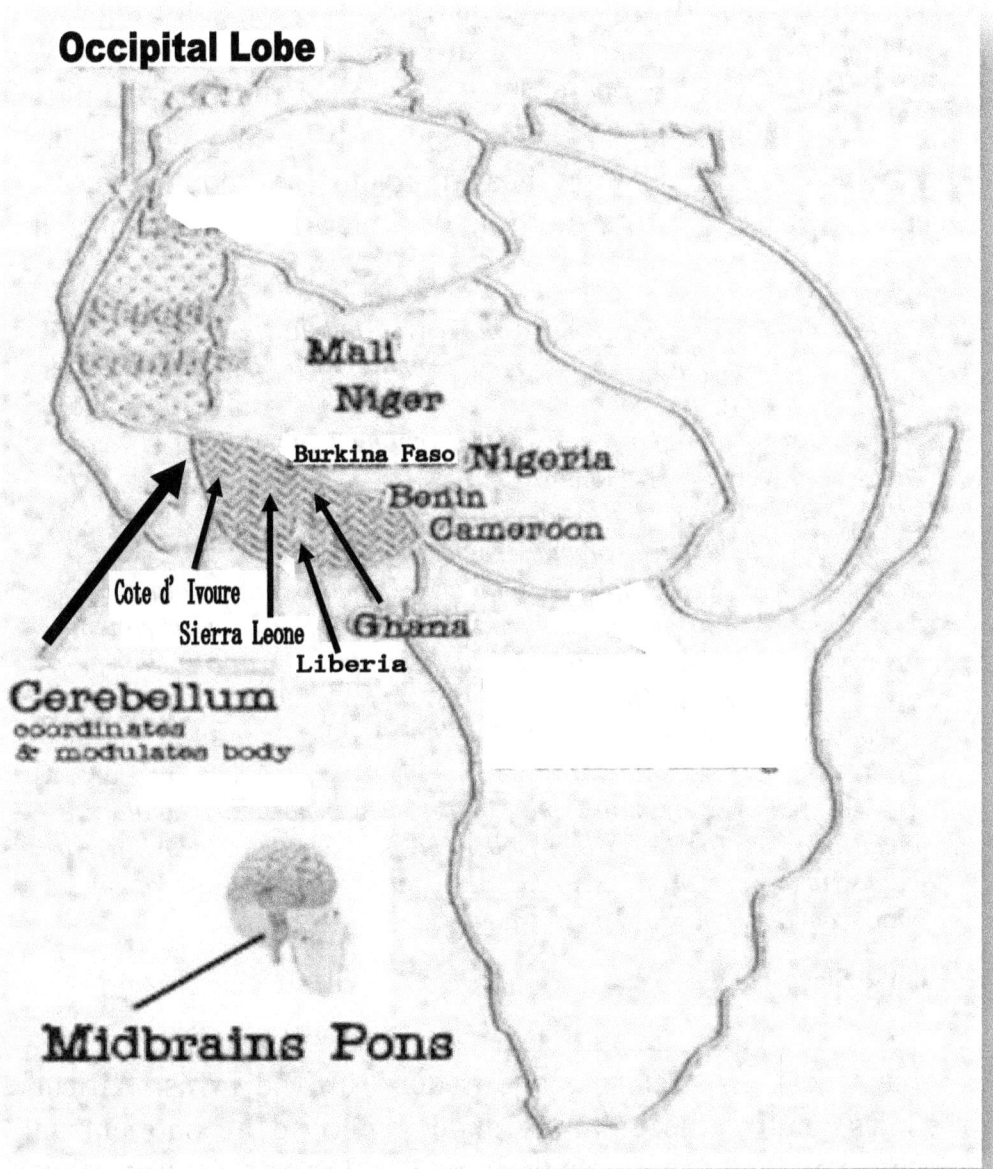

Without going into every detail regarding the value of each region in West Africa and the work that its ancient people performed within the cerebellum area, let us just say: The Black nation is very special in the eye sight of All Mighty God whose proper name is Allah—the creator of the Universe!

Of course, today Africa's once great people and civilizations' are dysfunctional and seem to be suffering from some form of brain damage. Can Africa be healed? "Yes she can"! How? By re-acquiring self-knowledge, re-gain the knowledge in all fields of science and lastly war no more against her own self. Africa can be healed, healthy and control its own wealth as it were during the time of Mansa Musa. Except more wisely.

> *"When the famous emperor of Mali, Mansa Musa visited Cairo in 1324, it was said that he brought so much gold with him that its price fell dramatically and had not recovered its value even 12 years later. The empire of Songhay was known, amongst other things, for the famous university of Sankore based in Timbuktu. Aristotle was studied at Sankore and also subjects such as law, various branches of philosophy, dialectic, grammar, rhetoric and astronomy. In the 16th century one of its most famous scholars, Ahmed Baba, is said to have written more than 40 major books on subjects such as astronomy, history and theology and he had his own private library that held over 1500 volumes. One of the first reports of Timbuktu to reach Europe was by Leo Africanus. In his book, published in 1550, he says of the town: 'There you will find many judges, professors and devout men, all handsomely maintained by the king, who holds scholars in much honour. There too they sell many handwritten North African books, and more profit is to be made there from the sale of books than from any other branch of trade.'"[49]*

Atlantic Slave Trade

E. Richard Capt author of *"The Great Pyramid Decoded"*, wrote "the trans-Atlantic slave trade destroyed [West African] peoples' and whole cultures; underdeveloped a continent and changed it forever; enriched Europe and created empires; and built the United States." [6]

One hundred million of slaves were brought to the Americas in slave ships beginning from the 1500's to the 1800's. For all intents and purposes, without the presence of

---

[49] www.antislavery.org/breakingthesilence/main/briefings/1.%20Africa%20before%20the%20Transatlantic%20Slave%20Trade.doc

African people in North America, the U.S.A. would have been hopeless long ago to boast as the wealthiest nation on earth! You might ask your self what were Caucasian American religious and political leaders thinking when they illegally allowed chattel slavery within her borders to continue 400 years. Did not they understand the words of the Bible {Revelator 18:11-13} who wrote:

> *"The merchants of the earth will weep and mourn over her because no one buys their cargoes any more— cargoes of gold, silver, precious stones and pearls; fine linen, purple, silk and scarlet cloth; every sort of citron wood, and articles of every kind made of ivory, costly wood, bronze, iron and marble; cargoes of cinnamon and spice, of incense, myrrh and frankincense, of wine and olive oil, of fine flour and wheat; cattle and sheep; horses and carriages; and* **slaves and souls of men***. Rejoice over her, O heaven! Rejoice, saints and apostles and prophets! God has judged her for the way she treated you." (Revelator 18:11-13)*

Why did America's forefathers repeat a worst history than ancient Babylon and *Biblical Egypt*? Will America be acquitted for repeating such a criminal act? Is there a price to pay called reparations for such a crime or does President Barak Obama represent payment enough? Judgment on this matter belongs wholly with Allah and his angels as it is written in both Bible and Qur'an (Rev 18; Holy Qur'an 15:20). Nevertheless, that does not mean none may speak or write on these matters with great zeal!

> *" Nay, We [نَحْن nahnu] hurl the Truth against falsehood, and it knocks out its brain, and behold, falsehood doth perish! Ah! woe be to you for the (false) things ye ascribe (to Us)" (Holy Qu'an 21: 18)*

The divine way in which nations are judged is not on an individual case basis. It's a national rendering as all nations bear just and unjust people of all persuasions regardless of race, color or greed. So again, Judgment belongs wholly with Allah and his angels.

CHAPTER 8

Vision Lost In West Africa

Western Sahara, Senegal and Gambia are located at the back of the geographical brain map in a region called occipital lobe, which regulates vision. The occipital lobes are the center of our visual perception system. They are not particularly vulnerable to injury because of their location at the back of the brain although any significant trauma to the brain could produce subtle changes to our visual-perceptual system, such as visual field defects and scotomas i.e., blind areas.

The peristriate region of the occipital lobe is involved in visuospatial processing, discrimination of movement and color discrimination...Disorders of the occipital lobe can cause visual hallucinations and illusions. Visual hallucinations (visual images with no external stimuli) can be caused by lesions to the occipital region or temporal lobe seizures. Visual illusions (distorted perceptions) can take the form of objects appearing larger or smaller than they actually are, objects lacking color or objects having abnormal coloring. Lesions in the parietal-temporal-occipital association area can cause word blindness with writing impairments.[50] (See Illustration VII)

Although Western Sahara, Senegal and Gambia's locale is in West Africa's geographical occipital area, Mauritania once dominated this area. After reading a brief overview of the history of what happened in Mauritania, you will understand how its invaders affected the west. You'll realize how West Africa lost its sight and vision long before they could grow in strength evermore.

"The most powerful of the tribes of the Sahara to the Sénégal River was the Lamtuna, whose culture of origin was 'Wadi Noun' (Nul Lemta). The Lamtuna are a Berber tribe from the region of Mauritania-Western Sahara-Morocco-Algeria. They claim descent

---

[50] http://www.neuroskills.com/tbi/boccipit.shtml

from Himyar, one of the South Arabian eponyms. The Himyarite Kingdom or anciently called Homerite Kingdom by the Greeks and the Romans, was a state in ancient South Arabia dating from 110 BC.

Illustration VII

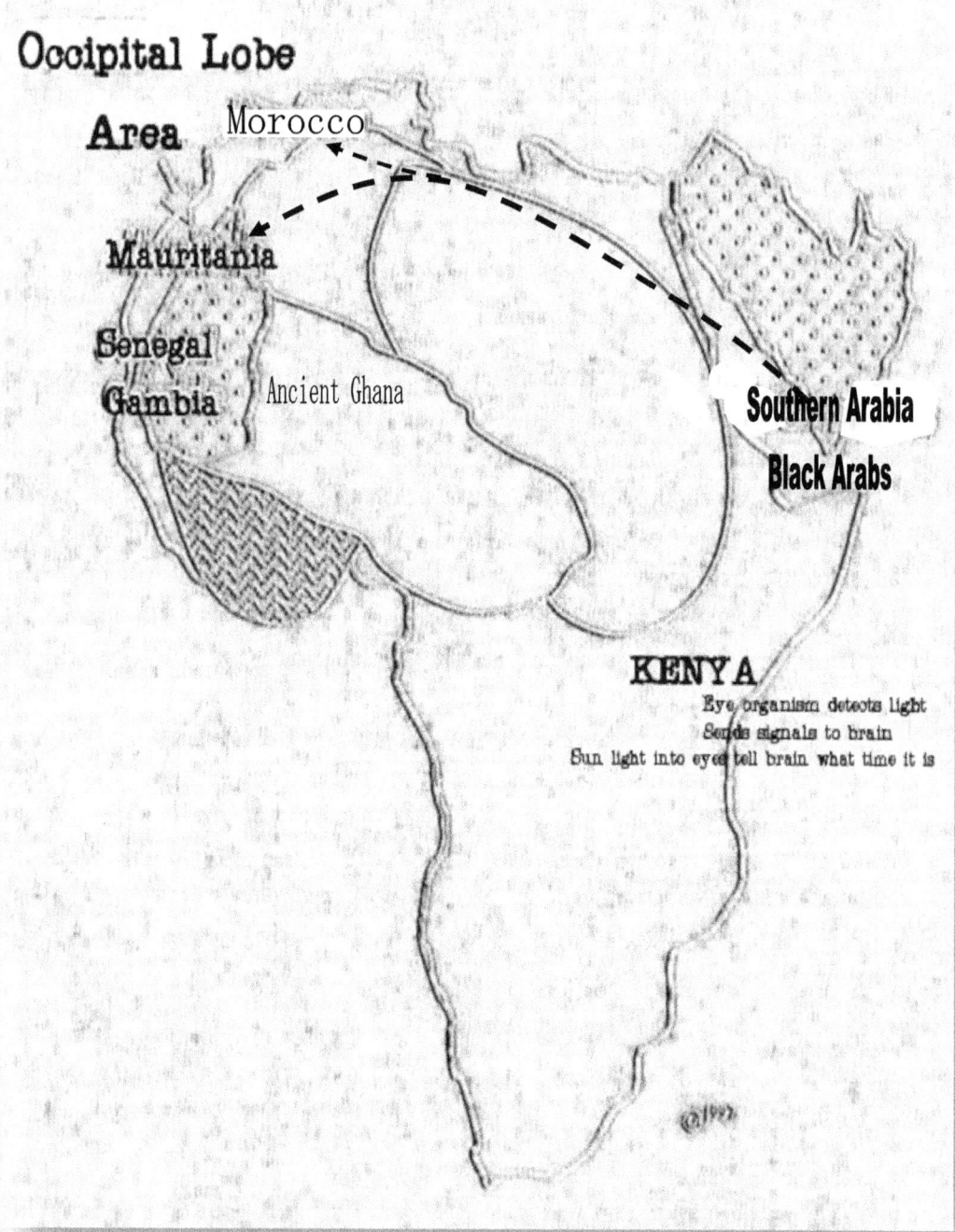

"From the 3rd to 7th century, the migration of Berber tribes from North Africa displaced the Bafours, the original inhabitants of present-day Mauritania and the ancestors of the Soninké. Continued Arab-Berber migration drove indigenous black Africans south to the Senegal River or enslaved them. By 1076, Islamic warriors (the Almoravid or Al Murabitun) completed the conquest of southern Mauritania, defeating the ancient Ghana Empire, only to go on to form the ruling dynasty in Morocco and Muslim Spain, to the north.[51]

Were it not for warfare within this region of West Africa's occipital lobe—Mauritania—perhaps certain tribes may have fought to prevent the Atlantic slave trade; in particularly, the Soninke' tribe, founders of the Ghana Empire.

"The Ghana Empire began when the Soninke people joined forces to resist the raids of pastoral nomads...During times of drought, the nomads would raid the villages to the south in search of water and pastures for their herds. To protect themselves from these raids, the communities of African farmers joined forces, possibly to form a loose federation of states that eventually became the kingdom of Ghana... Rulers of the state kept extending their borders in order to gain control of the trade routes by conquering neighboring territories. By the fifth century, the Soninke kingdom of Ghana had been established. This kingdom lasted about six centuries before being conquered by new forces from the east...However; it was control of the gold fields in the southwest that was essential to Ghana's political control and economic prosperity. The location of these goldfields was kept strictly secret by the Soninke. By the tenth century, Ghana was an immensely rich and prosperous empire, probably controlling an area the size of Texas or Nigeria in what is now eastern Senegal, southwest Mali, and southern Mauritania. The ruler was acclaimed as the "richest king in the world because of his gold" by Arab traveler Ibn Haukal, who visited the region in about 950 A.D. Demand for gold increased in the ninth and tenth centuries for minting into coins by the Islamic states of North Africa. As the trans-Saharan trade in gold expanded, so did the state of Ghana. The trans-Sahara trade also brought Islam to the empire, initially to the rulers and townspeople...In the eleventh century, shortly after Ghana reached its zenith, the city of Kumbi Saleh fell to

---

[51] http://en.wikipedia.org/wiki/Almoravid

the Berber Almoravids (1076), who swept across the desert from present-day Mauritania in an effort to control the gold trade and to purify Islam, as it was practiced in Ghana. The invaders subsequently withdrew, but the kingdom of Ghana was weakened. Later invasions by the Takrur people from the west (the Senegal valley) and others, together with secessionist movements from many rebellious sub-kingdoms which had previously paid regular tribute to the Ghanaian king, gradually made the trade routes through Ghana too dangerous. As a result, the Muslim merchants moved eastward, and with the loss of trade, the kingdom of Ghana began to crumble. In addition, in the eleventh and twelfth centuries, the Bure goldfields were opened up to the south, also drawing traders further east. A terrible drought further compounded the suffering and accelerated the deterioration of the environment--degradation that was probably accentuated also by overgrazing. By the mid-thirteenth century, the once great empire of Ghana had disintegrated.[52]

War caused damage to this geographical area of West Africa in terms of its parietal-temporal-occipital association. (Review Illustration VII) Certainly its long-term stability and vision toward future development and self-defense were impaired. What happened in Mauritania evinces how this particular area was severely damaged by warfare, Berber invaders and ironically Middle Eastern Muslims from the holy land. Nevertheless, it was all for a reason and a season.

The perceived travesty of time against the ancient rule of the Black nation was really a blessing and a mercy in disguise. But the mercy would be for the development of the people of Jacob (Yacub) who would come to mediate (police) between aboriginal warring tribes and nations that could stymie them from an ultimate internal war against itself. Bottom line: Until such time when Black men war no more against self and kind, Caucasians rule by default.

However, a vital sign of the rise of the Black nation may now be near at hand based upon a recent article in the Final Call Newspaper. After reading this article, it seems Africa is poised

---

[52] http://mali.pwnet.org/history/history_ghana_empire.htm

to regain control over itself to re-establish its global presence as a United States of Africa and insistently war no more.

"TRIPOLI, Libya (FinalCall.com) - The African Union (AU) summit in the Ethiopian capital Addis Ababa recently elected the Leader of the Libyan Revolution Muammar Gadhafi new President of the AU. The position will give Gadhafi the power to influence policies across Africa for the next year. Gadhafi immediately vowed to push on with his plans to strengthen the institutions of the AU and make the African states stronger, stable and peaceful in a rather unstable world.

"In his acceptance speech, he said, "I think the coming time will be a time of serious work and a time for action, not just empty words." He told Africa's heads of state that there is much to do and that some of AU procedures need to be reviewed in order to speed up the establishment of African Union institutions.

"He also promised to do all he can to solve the problem of Darfur and other African conflicts. In his acceptance speech, Gadhafi acknowledged that he, at times, provoked some of Africa's heads of state in order to push the agenda of the African Union.

"However, he said, for the African leaders to have different views regarding the future of the content is healthy. Credit goes to all heads of state and their sovereign countries for making the right decisions, said the Libyan leader. It was reported that in a closed meeting much of the opposition to the election of Gadhafi was lead by South Africa and Uganda, two countries that the Libyan Leader and his country's men and women had helped the most to achieve their goals of freedom and justice for their people.

"Gadhafi told the summit he did not wish to take up the post of the chairman of the AU earlier, even though he was invited to, because he believed that his position was to help push the car regardless who was the driver. Africa must realize its dreams of unity, regardless of any one's official position.

"Gadhafi is, in fact, the engineer and the founder of the AU. He called for an emergency African Summit of the Organization of African Unity on Sept. 9, 1999 in Libya, and methodically laid out why the OAU should move forward African Union. He said if Dr. Kwame Nkrumah could rise from his grave, the masses, the young,

the old, the students, the workers, the military, the civil servants and the politicians would have carried him on their shoulders. The African masses' real objective is to see the birth of a United States of Africa that is rich, peaceful and secure...

*"Gadhafi believes with so many other Leaders of Africa, as well as millions of Africans in the Diaspora, that only a **United States of Africa** can tackle the long-term issues of poverty, disease, illiteracy, and conflicts and make the continent a global powerhouse. He recognized, however, that there was much work to be done and that many African leaders are not in agreement with where and how to start.*

In his closing speech, Gadhafi made it clear that Libya alone among oil-producing nations has not lost money during the world financial crisis. "Libya has not lost a single dollar in this crisis. Libya has invested billions in Africa. We have not invested in America," he emphasized.

"Gadhafi praised the new American president and described Barack Hussein Obama's accession to the White House as a victory against racism, and urged the first Black U.S. president to lead his country boldly and with integrity. "The Black people's struggle has made tremendous advances against racism in America. It was God who created color. Today President Obama, a son of Kenyan father, a true son of Africa, has made it in the United States of America," he said".[53]

As President Obama travels the globe influencing policies for other nations' and peoples' economic well being, let us hope him and the first lady; from their profound stature, will ultimately muster the wherewithal to influence *AFRICA'S* economic well being. After all it has always been known that African resources represent the final investment frontier! In fact, according to an article in Forbes Magazine entitled, **"Africa: The Last Investment Frontier.'** It reads:

"Capital markets are the lifeblood of economic development. Without deep, liquid markets, it's hard for any country or region--developed or emerging--to reach its full potential. While Africa still has a long

---

[53] http://www.finalcall.com/artman/publish/article_5674.shtml

way to go, it has made some promising strides in developing its equity markets: In 1989, there were just five sub-Saharan stock exchanges; now there are 16...

"Part of the reason for the excitement is that the economies of sub-Saharan Africa are in the best shape in several decades. Africa is on track to deliver economic growth of nearly 7% in 2008. Inflation, which measures below 7%, is high by the standards of the developed world, but nowhere near crisis levels. Record oil prices have certainly helped stabilize African economies, but the International Monetary Fund notes that improvements have also been broad-based, attributable to better macroeconomic policies in recent years.

"As it turns out, Kenya has been a much better place to park your money in this year's market turmoil than the Dow Jones. Stocks in Nairobi are up 5% year-to-date, vs. double-digit plunges in the U.S. and Europe and even sharper declines in last year's market darlings, China and India.

*"Overall, **Morgan Stanley's** (nyse: MS - news - people) Capital International Africa index, which tracks the performance of Kenya, Mauritius, Nigeria and Tunisia, is off 4% since the start of 2008, vs. a 15% plunge in MSCI's emerging market index.*

*"While African stocks remain mainly an institutional game, even small investors are able to tap into the region's growth through the **T. Rowe Price Africa and Middle East Fund** (nasdaq: TRAMX - news - people), launched last September. The **SPDR S&P Emerging Middle East & Africa** (nyse: GAF - news - people) exchange-traded fund is another option.*

"Investors have good reason to be optimistic about Africa's long-term prospects, but plenty of work remains to be done. In a briefing last year, the African Partnership Forum outlined a number of specific goals, ranging from simplified labor laws to cracking down on corruption and improving political stability. Africa's high cost of doing business and low savings rates must also be addressed.

"These are not issues that will be easily resolved over sushi at a Japanese resort. And there is clearly a more pressing need to help

Africa reach the Millennium Development Goals by 2015. But there's no reason the G-8 leaders can't aim even higher.[54]

So in terms of African peoples' self-determination to manifest a continental self-governance, it's all up to them and Black America to link once-and-for all to organize their human and material resources in a most excellent, intelligent economic growth process.

"Allah does not change the condition of any people, unless they themselves make the decision to change... "(Quran 13:11)

Kenya The Eye of Africa

When one considers the profile of Africa as a human skull, Kenya is located exactly where our eye sockets are fixed. (Review Illustration VII on pg. 90) Therefore, let us bear in mind a terrible decease of the eye that no one hopes to suffer. It is called Strabismus (from Greek: στραβισμός *strabismos* "to squint," from στραβός *strabos* "squinting") or a condition in which the eyes are not properly aligned with each other. It typically involves a lack of coordination between the extraocular muscles that prevents bringing the gaze of each eye to the same point in space and preventing proper binocular vision, which may adversely affect depth perception.[55]

Strabismus or squint eye can also be a disorder of the brain coordinating the eyes. Hence, the Holy Quran says of squint eyed people:

*"**The day when the trumpet is blown; and We shall gather the guilty, blue-eyed or squint eye, on that day, Consulting together secretly: You tarried but ten (days). We know best what they say when the fairest of them in course would say: You tarried but a day.** And they ask thee about the mountains. Say: My Lord will scatter them, as scattered dust, Then leave it a plain, smooth, level, Wherein thou seest no crookedness nor unevenness. On that day they will*

---

[54] http://www.forbes.com/2008/07/05/economies-stocks-investment-pf-summit08-cx_jhc_0707africa.html

[55] http://en.wikipedia.org/wiki/Strabismus

follow the Inviter, in whom is no crookedness; and the voices are low before the Beneficent God, so that thou hearest naught but a soft sound. On that day no intercession avails except of him whom the Beneficent allows, and whose word He is pleased with. He knows what is before them and what is behind them, while they cannot comprehend it in knowledge. And faces shall be humbled before the Living, the Self-subsistent. And he who bears iniquity is indeed undone. (Holy Quran 20:102-111)

A United States of Africa absolutely represents a hub for all Black people throughout the Diaspora first and foremost as a native homeland! Let us hope none of the African Union members will allow the guilty blue eyes to cause them to suffer from squint eye and loose sight of the value of a united continent of Africa!

CHAPTER 9

Islam Resurrected Europe

The only African countries that rest in the geographical brain-maps Parietal Lobe region are Morocco, Tunisia, Algeria and parts of the Western Sahara. Hardly do we ever here about any news events coming out of Morocco, Algeria or Western Sahara. Who are these people? What greatness have they manifested in ancient times or modern times? These countries are located in the parietal lobe positioned above (superior to) the occipital lobe and behind (posterior to) the frontal lobe. It integrates sensory information from different modalities, particularly determining spatial sense and navigation— intuition.

The parietal lobe plays an important role in integrating sensory information from various parts of the body, knowledge of numbers and their relations, and in the manipulation of objects. Portions of the parietal lobe are involved with visuospatial processing—capability to perceive.[56] Much less is known about this lobe than the other three in the cerebrum. (See Illustration VIII)

In terms of the parietal lobes parallel relationship with Morocco, northwest Africa, this territories geographical global-brain position is responsible for **intuition** (sense and navigation) usually connected to our ability to perceive or know immediately without reasoning, which is often regarded as a divine or prophetic power viz., nature of PARIETAL LOBE!

The word 'intuition' comes from the Latin word *'intueri'*, which is often roughly translated as meaning *'to look inside'* or *'to contemplate'*. Intuition provides us with beliefs that we cannot necessarily justify. For this reason, it has been the subject of study in psychology, as well as a topic of interest in the supernatural. The *"right brain"* is popularly associated with intuitive processes such as aesthetic abilities. According to

---

[56] http://en.wikipedia.org/wiki/Parietal_lobe

Historical and Cultural Perspectives pg. 97 Gerald Holton contends that intuition is associated with innovation in scientific discovery.

Illustration VIII

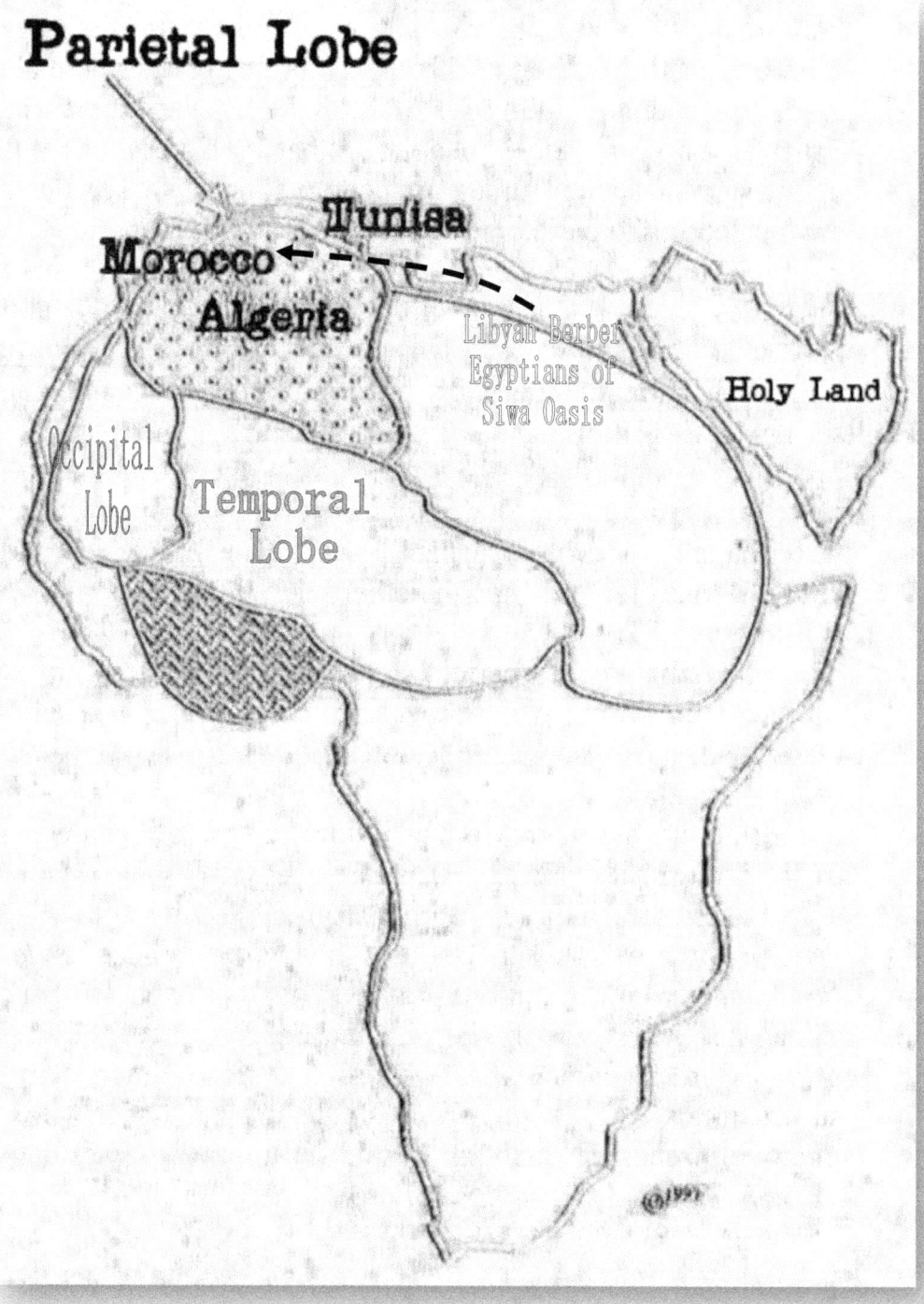

"Many invaders and colonists reached the Maghreb (North Africa), including Phoenicians, Romans, Vandals, Byzantines, Arabs, Turks and French.

"The name Berber evolved from the Greek custom of calling all non-Greek speaking people Barbarians. **The Berbers call themselves "Imazighen", the free.** *The Berbers originally lived all over the Maghreb (**Morocco**) from western Egypt to the Atlantic. The culturally distinct Berber communities of today survive in pockets in the mountains and in the Sahara desert, scattered over a large area from the Siwa Oasis in Egypt to the Atlantic and from the Niger river and the Sahel in the south to the Mediterranean. Their density increases from east to west, Morocco being the state with most Berbers living in it.*[57]

What I gather from the above history is that western Egypt's Imazighen (Libyan Berber) people and including Southern Arabia's Himyarites were sent to Morocco in advance to serve a Divine purpose. The question here becomes: How calamitous was northwest Africa damaged after the initial impact by foreign invaders? In retrospect, it does appear nothing was left to chance. Truth of matter is; in 711 A.D a Libyan Berber army led by general Tariq ibn Ziyad, invaded Iberia (Spain) from Morocco to overthrow the savage Visigoths (Western Goths)—one of two main branches of the Goths, an east Germanic tribe, who over the period of only one hundred years, had migrated from eastern Europe, thru Greece, thru Italy, and finally down into the Iberian peninsula (Spain).

"In Morocco came the next dynasty, from the south **The Almoravides.** *They were camel-riding Berber of the Sanhaja group of tribes, to whom cultivation of the soil was unknown. For a century or more they have been conquering and* **converting to Islam the black countries of the Sahara**, *inspired by their search for the source of gold which had been flowing into Morocco from somewhere in the region of the Niger river...*

"Much of Spain became part of the Almoravide Empire. *A period of peace and prosperity followed, enriched by the refined culture of the*

---

[57] http://www.angelfire.com/az/rescon/mgcberbr.html

Andalucian courts to which had been added a healthy dose of Berber virility and discipline.[58]

The **Almoravids** were a Berber dynasty from the Sahara that spread over a wide area of northwestern Africa and Spain. Under this dynasty the Moorish empire the map show its extension over present-day Morocco, Western Sahara, Mauritania, Gibraltar, Tlemcen (in Algeria) and a great part of what is now

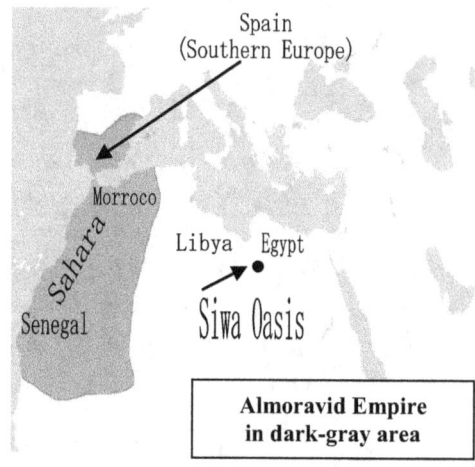

Senegal and Mali in the south, and Spain and Portugal to the north in Europe.

Overall, Berber Muslim (Moor) dynasties exercised varying degrees of power and political authority in Spain between 711 AD and 1492 AD, contributing to the scientific, cultural and intellectual progress, not only in southern Europe, but Western Europe as a whole. In southern Spain, Moors cultivated the arts and sciences, as well as the standards of etiquette and sanitation that rivaled any other European city of that day and age. The intellectual renown of Cordoba attracted knowledge-thirsty students from throughout Europe. Countless volumes of books on topics ranging from alchemy to algebra were housed in any of Cordoba's numerous libraries. When these texts were translated from Arabic, the language of commerce and learning, to European languages, Spain's neighbors were exposed to new scientific advances or reintroduced to old knowledge that had been long forgotten. With the arrival of the Moors in Spain, Europe witnessed for the first time an Islamic religious and cultural presence within its

---

[58] http://www.magicmorocco.com/history_of_morocco.html

borders that feed a viable challenge to Western Europe's concept of civilization, culture and faith.[59]

The Quran says, *"...**Those who prevailed said, 'We will build a place of worship around them....'"** (Quran 18:21)* It is my belief this verse represented a continuum of instructions for Muslims while in Morocco to keep Western Europe from collapsing. It was a mercy from Allah. Therefore Morocco was used as a launching pad by which religion (Islam) would enter into the Caucasian's world during its Dark Age period. When one is leading another out of darkness such as the Berber Moors did for Europe, effectively they were giving old Europe a new intuition—a look inside or contemplation—to which they'd lost during their days of civil, social and religious darkness or ignorance. Yes Black men put Caucasian men back in touch with the rest of the civilized ancient world by employing the principles of Islam. And while in Spain (southern Europe) they established institutions by which Western Europe was ultimately resurrected out of her societal failures into the age of administering the social and economic life of a renewed culture particularly around the 14th century.

The two images below show (1) a priceless jewelry named Blackamoor and (2) some ancient European currency with the image of a Moorish warrior.[60]

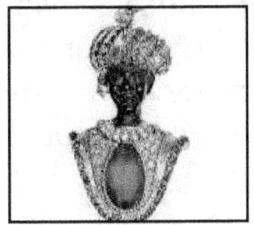 

Another analysis about the parietal lobe entails the Caspian culture (named after the town of Gafsa in Tunisia) since at least 10,000 BC. During this period, the environment was open savanna, much like modern East Africa, with

[59] http://wow.uab.edu/spain/show.asp?durki=29701
[60] http://jumamshabazi.webs.com/moorishmartialscience.htm

Mediterranean forests at higher altitudes. Anatomically, Caspian populations were modern Homo sapiens [Black people]…Some have argued that they were immigrants from the east, whereas others argue for population continuity based on physical skeletal characteristics and other criteria.[61]

In 1100 BC the Phoenicians influenced the region. Around 200 BC, the Kingdom of Numidia was established by Massinissa, who operated as an ally of Rome, motivated by the growing force of Carthage (today's Tunisia). During the 400 AD, economic decline in the Roman Empire resulted in a dramatic fall in revenues in Numidia. In 430 AD, Vandals destroyed the Roman rule in North Africa, and the region is dissolved into many small kingdoms. In 534 AD, Algeria is conquered by Emperor Justinian I, and becomes a part of the East Roman Empire (what would become the Byzantine Empire). In 670 AD, Arab conquest occurs in Algeria. In spite of all these conquests, the language of Algeria's population belongs to the Afro-Asiatic language family and it can be broken down into 300 different dialects.

Algeria's boundaries have shifted during various stages of its conquests; the French, whose colonization began in 1830, created its modern borders. Indigenous Algerians began their revolt on November 1, 1954; to gain rights denied them under French rule. On March 1962, French citizens living in Algeria at the time, called the "pieds-noirs," left Algeria for France. So once again, we read of apparent historical conflicts within the PARIETAL LOBE region, except this one happened in Algeria.

Neurologists know that a lesion to the posterior parietal cortex leads to a loss of body scheme, so that the patient denies a profound left hemiparesis, neglects stimuli to the left side of the body, and even denies that the left side of their body is their own. Such deficits are much more common with right hemisphere lesions than with left. Neurologists also say damage to the *[Parietal lobe]* can cause visuo-spatial deficits, that is, (1)

---

[61] http://en.wikipedia.org/wiki/Capsian_culture

the patient may have difficulty finding their way around new, or even familiar places and (2) may disrupt a patient's ability to understand spoken and/or written language. [7]

With regard to the Berber people of North Africa, it appears that history elevates them as having not denied the  people on the left side because Europe was shown Allah's mercy through His servants—Berber Blackamoors. More evidence will be shown in chapter 9 how North African Berbers sense of intuition was not ruined in spite of its many foreign invaders.

Modern Berbers - ancient Libyans known as Lebu/Libu, Meshwesh, and later as Moors

All that can be said here is that Mother Africa (Black nation) must no longer deprive herself from high sciences and principles of righteousness derived as of Islam. Considering her incalculable civilizations' produced by Islamic principles, to borrow a phrase…"the world is ours."

In summation, yes the descendants of the Original Black nation of the globe were dumb downed over many centuries. It is as if their ancient God intelligence, mental power and capability were frozen, except a small circle of leaders described as the 12 Imams or scientists. But stagnation was allowed by very wise scientists of the Original nation to enable Caucasians to produce their circle of ruling monarchs. For that reason, the Original nation metaphorically fainted for a season and for a reason. The Honorable Elijah Muhammad herein gave the unadulterated explanation:

> *"If Islam had been forced upon all the people of the earth during the past 6000 years there would not have been any 'world of Christianity,' there would not have been any 'World of Buddhism,'… and there would never have been anything like 'The Caucasian World.' Islam would have prevented their progress. God Himself has held Islam 'in check' to give these other 'worlds' free reign during the past 6000 years."* **[Elijah Muhammad Dec. 1960 Vol. 1, No. 4 edition of Muhammad Speaks Newspaper]**

The process to healing Africa's (as well as Black America) mental ills or socio-geographical problems is equivalent to healing a patient with brain lobe injuries. In view of that, healing begins with neurologic rehabilitation. This form of rehabilitation must be dedicated to education and vocational services to both children and adults. Through the provision of individualized assessment, restorative service and foundational retraining in behavior, psych-social, cognitive, physical functioning, communication and daily living, Mother Africa's ancient descendants will attain a maximum level of functioning and quality of life in the most normalized and least restrictive environment.

Of course, it will cost billions of dollars, but it is worth every ounce of Gold in Fort Knox, operated by the U.S. Treasury Department, to restore the Black Nation from America to Africa as it took Billions to destroy this once noble people.

"Here in America there are also three and one-half million indirect believers in Islam, in the secret order called Shriners, or Higher Masons. When you take the 33-degree in masonry you are no longer called a Mason; you are then called a Moslem Son, and in that order (or degree) you are taught the prayers of the Moslems and you come under the teachings of Islam. In that High Degree you are taught to turn your face eastward, toward the Holy City of Mecca in Arabia. All of this is part of the Moslem religion, Islam that we know what is in store for this world; we know what tomorrow will bring.

"Why do we call God a Divine Being? Because He is like we are but His wisdom, power, and other capabilities and attributes are Supreme...making Him the Highest Power, the Supreme in Power, or Supreme Power. He is a being like ourselves, but He has the Divine Capacity of exercising His Power or to project through His Power the powers of the Universe...and therefore we call Him the Supreme Being and the God of the Universe. He has the Divine Power to will whatever He wishes and to bring it into existence with His Divine

Will. But He is not an invisible spirit somewhere up in the Sky. His home is right here on this earth. [62]

Higher Masons (Moslem sons) understand such essential knowledge about God. They waste no time investing to make their imaginations' patent. Furthermore, they also recognize the symbol shown below which is placed at the upper ceiling of many shrines wherein they learn Islam in secret. I personally saw this symbol

Moroccan-style facade
Los Angeles Shrine Auditorium

(along with Brother Stanley Muhammad of Mosque #27) on the ceiling of the Los Angeles Shrine Auditorium in 1985. I recall Brother Stanley and I making a security check in a particular room before Minister Farrakhan spoke there. As we looked above our heads, behold we saw this symbol which bear witness to the father of civilization.

---

[62] http://www.muhammadspeaks.com/MessengerinAtlanta.html

So as we looked up, suddenly one fellow yelled, *"hey! Get out of here"*! Of course, we immediately exited the room respecting those in authority of the facility. Later that evening, as FARRAKHAN spoke, above the audience hovered a Divine ancient symbol of themselves only this time covered-over by a beautiful embroidered silk quilt pinned down by a dangling lit chandelier. In any event, Higher Masons know who and what the Black nation has represented!

CHAPTER 10

The Libyan Connection

Inscriptions found in Egypt dating from the Old Kingdom (2700-2200 B.C.) are the earliest known recorded testimony of the Berber migration and also the earliest written documentation of Libyan history. At least as early as this period, troublesome Berber tribes, one of which was identified in Egyptian records as the Levu (or "Libyans"), were raiding eastward as far as the Nile Delta and attempting to settle there.

During the Middle Kingdom (2200-1700 B.C.) the Egyptian pharaohs succeeded in imposing their overlordship on these eastern Berbers and extracted tribute from them. Many Berbers served in the army of the pharaohs, and some rose to positions of importance in the Egyptian state. One such Berber officer seized control of Egypt in about 950 B.C. and, as Shishonk I, ruled as pharaoh. His successors of the twenty-second and twenty-third Bubastite dynasties—the so-called Libyan dynasties of 945-730 B.C.—are also believed to have been Berbers.[63]

Sheshonq I

Sheshonq II

Who are these mysterious people referred to as Berbers that seem to have been marked by breaks or interruptions distributed from the Atlantic to the Siwa oasis, in Egypt, and from the Mediterranean to the Niger River. With a bit more research, you shall see who the Berbers are. (Review map on pg. 98)

---

[63] http://www.somalipress.com/libya-overview/history-ancient-libya-1083.html

Up to now we have dealt with Africa's geographical cerebellum, frontal, parietal and occipital lobes to illustrate how they relate to the psychology of her ancient people. We also traced some of the spiritual problems afflicting the globe of the original people in terms of how the nature of earths constructs functions internally and externally.

Now we shall examine Libya—land of the *"free humans"* (Berbers) to see how this North African country fits into the divine geographical scheme of things. But let us first recall for a moment in 1986 when former U.S. President, Ronald Reagan and the late Pope John Paul II, sanctioned the bombing of Libya in an attempt to murder the former Libyan leader, Colonel Muammar El Qahdafi. Although he survived this *"bombing"* assassination, it cost U.S. taxpayers one billion dollars to pay for the attack code-named Operation *El Dorado Canyon.* Therefore, I reiterate, who are the Berbers? I pose this question because the Honorable Minister Louis Farrakhan went to <u>Libya</u> to warn the Colonel of America's attack before it occurred, thus possibly sparing his life.

The *"Berber"* people of Libya have been proven friends of the Nation of Islam since 1972. Bear in mind it was Colonel El Qahdafi, who first awarded the Nation of Islam and the Honorable Elijah Muhammad 4.5 million dollars to purchase the largest Temple of Islam in Chicago, Illinois 1972. Then in 1988 Libya loaned the Nation of Islam and the Honorable Minister Louis Farrakhan a 5 million dollar interest-free loan.

Then again, in 1996 after Louis Farrakhan's visit to Libya, *"The free peoples of Libya"* offered him $250,000 dollars, some say 1 Billion dollars; others said up to 10 Billion. But the real truth of the matter is as follows:

August 30, 1996 Web posted at: 8:30 p.m. EDT (0030 GMT)

TRIPOLI, Libya (CNN) -- In a dramatic about-face, Louis Farrakhan told Libya he accepts the "honor" of a human rights award, but cannot accept the $250,000 that goes with the prize without the approval of a U.S. court.

"I will accept the honor of this prize but I will ask you to hold the monies until a decision is made by a (U.S.) court of law," Farrakhan told an enthusiastic audience in the Libyan capital.

The Nation of Islam leader had vowed earlier this week to "go across the nation" rallying support, if the government did not allow him to accept the prize.

But on Wednesday, the U.S. Treasury Department denied Farrakhan's request that he be exempted from U.S. sanctions requiring banks under U.S. jurisdiction to freeze transactions relating to Libya.

If convicted of violating the sanctions -- or of conspiring to do so -- Farrakhan could have faced a prison sentence and fines.

Justifying its rejection of the request, the treasury agency said Libya has been on Washington's list of states that sponsor international terrorism since December 1979. Libya is under U.N. sanctions, imposed in 1992, to force it to surrender two men wanted in the 1988 bombing of a Pan Am jet over Lockerbie, Scotland, that killed 270 people.

The U.S. has also sought to further isolate Tripoli with recent legislation that punishes non-U.S. companies with major investments in Libya.

As a result of the relationship between Libya and the Nation of Islam in North America, some in the U.S. government proposed to further ruin it by introducing a Bill to the 104th CONGRESS, 2d Session, **H. RES. 365,** condemning [the] visit by the Honorable Minister Louis Farrakhan to Libya, Iran, and Iraq as well as certain statements he made during those visits, and urged President Regan to take appropriate action to determine if such visits, statements, and actions resulting from agreements or understandings reached during these visits violate Federal law.

IN THE HOUSE OF REPRESENTATIVES

February 27, 1996

Mr. LANTOS (for himself and Mr. KING) submitted the following resolution; which was referred to the Committee on International Relations

Resolved, That the House of Representatives—
  (1) condemns the visit of Louis Farrakhan to Libya, Iran, and Iraq;

  (2) condemns statements made by Mr. Farrakhan during those visits which are derogatory of the foreign policy of the United States and which support the governments of these countries, all of which are on the list of countries which support terrorism; and

  (3) calls upon the President to direct appropriate Federal government agencies to determine if any United States laws were violated by Mr. Farrakhan by these visits or in statements made by him during these visits or in actions which result from agreements or understandings reached during these visits, and, if so, actively to prosecute any such violations of United States law.

This Bill to the 104th CONGRESS, 2d Session, H. RES. 365 gives authority to the words written by the Honorable Elijah Muhammad May 19, 1972 in the Muhammad Speaks Newspaper wherein he said: "THE white people of America are so wicked against helping the Black once-slave that if they hear that a foreigner wants to help us, the white American goes and tries to prevent foreigners from helping us! THIS SHOWS how hateful and evil the children of the white race are in their evil desire to keep us a free slave and to prevent any foreign help to come to us. THE white man likes to see us suffering for his help and he portions his help to us, such as a little food to eat, and a half-rotten and torn-down house to live in!"

For the record, Libya's people are just as special in their geographical brain locale of Mother Africa as all other African people. Libya is situated on a geographical global-brain position where it is influenced under what I see as the cerebral cortex.

(See Illustration IX) The cerebral cortex is a structure within the brain that plays a key role in memory, attention, perceptual awareness, thought, language, and consciousness.[64]

Maybe this explains why Libya was inspired by Allah's Divine Will to concern itself with the Nation of Islam in North America. Maybe this is why Libya is inspired to spearhead the movement for an African Union (United States of Africa). Maybe this is why Libya once upon a time involved its government resources with many "revolutionary" conscious movements that fought for freedom against imperialist agendas and oppression!

Libya & US Relations

From an all points bulletin Libya is still aware and conscious of freedom and perceptual awareness. For instance, U.S. news reported Secretary of State Condilizza Rice visits with  former enemy, Moammar Gadhafi and this was the first official travel to Libya by a U.S. Secretary of State since 1957. The headline read TRIPOLI, Libya - The U.S. and Libya sealed a historic turnaround in their troubled relations with a meeting Friday 5 September 2008 between Secretary of State Condoleezza Rice and Libyan leader Moammar Gadhafi. It appeared as if America was need of a helping hand from Libya to possibly regain consciousness and awareness about how to get free of debt. Then, sadly an order was issued to kill Moammar Gadhafi in 2012. So now, more cerebral cortex issues have been inflicted upon Mother Africa's [re]development.

"Rice's visit comes amid a surge in interest from U.S. companies, particularly in the energy sector, in doing business in Libya, where European companies have had much greater access in recent years. Libya's proven oil reserves are the ninth largest in the world, close to 39 billion barrels, and vast areas remain unexplored.

---

[64] http://en.wikipedia.org/wiki/Cerebral_cortex

Think this over!

"New development of energy supplies has worldwide importance, Rice said, but 'the relationship has much broader potential than just energy.'

"White House press secretary Dana Perino said Friday in Washington that the Bush administration hopes to announce a new ambassador there soon. 'We have had a long and bad history with Libya,' she said. 'That began to turn around when they turned away from nuclear weapons and terrorism. That country has radically changed its behavior and Secretary Rice's trip signifies a new chapter in U.S.-Libya bilateral relations.'"

Illustration IX

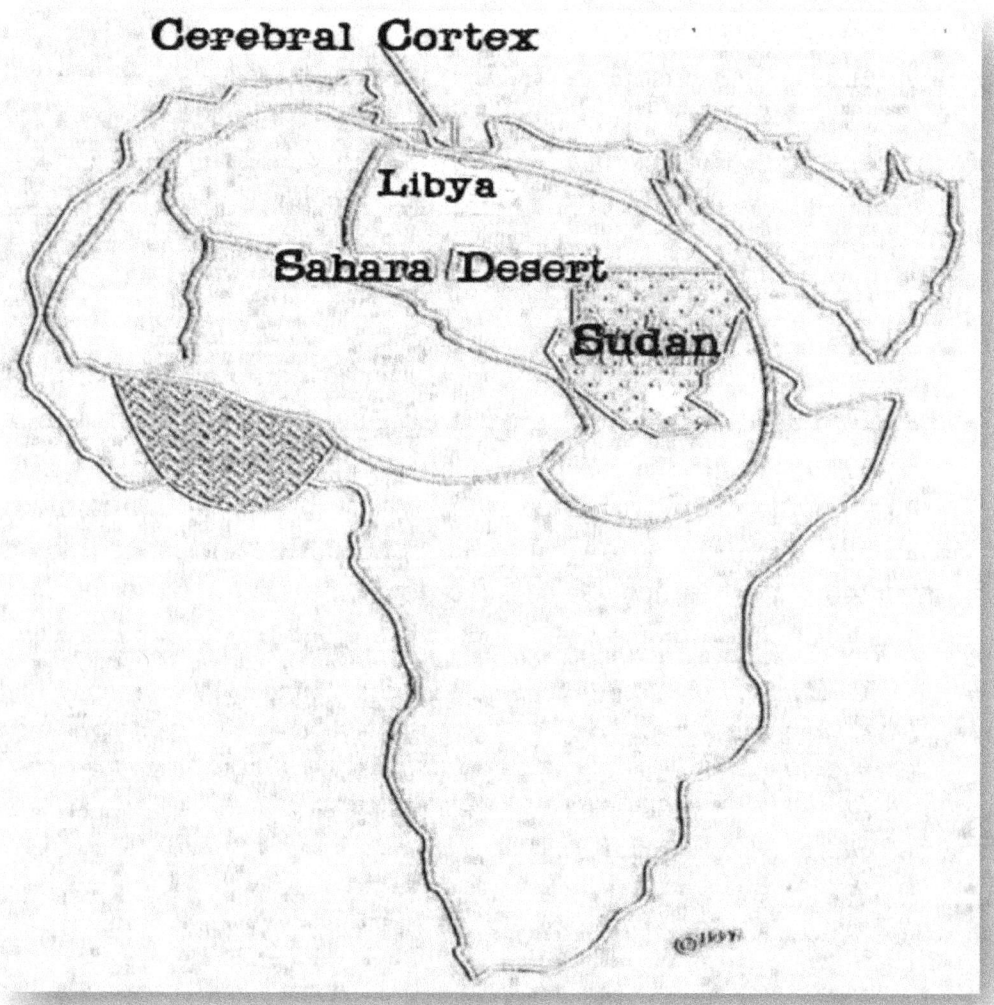

Africa definitely holds the key to future worldwide economic stability. The question is: Does Africa know that it holds the key. And if she knows, with who will Africa call in Black America when time arrives to negotiate and rewrite foreign policy between the two people—Black and white. Fact is the entire world, including China and Arabia, need African land, resources and minerals to continue with their upward mobility!

God willing (Inshallah), Black America and Black Africa will unite with intelligence to prevent another 1884–85 Berlin Conference, during which time Africa's resources were regulated under absolute European Imperialistic control.

CHAPTER 11

Message To The Black Man

When you look at the silhouette of Europe and America, a flying dragon with a head seems to sit atop both massive bodies of land. Particularly Europe, with her captive allies (i.e. *China, Russia, India, Arabia and the Middle East*), which also seem to hover above Mother Africa as if to prey upon her inhabitants and resources.

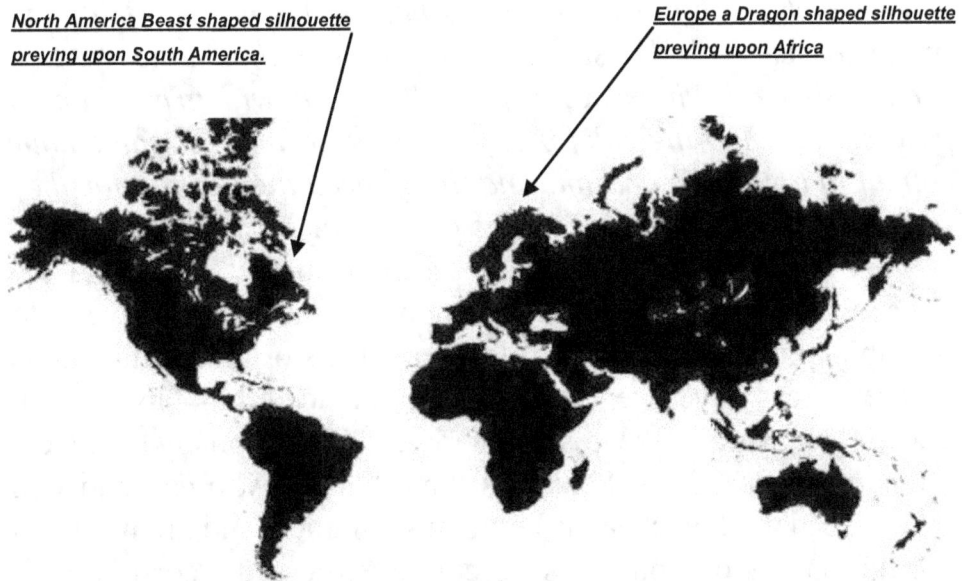

North America Beast shaped silhouette preying upon South America.

Europe a Dragon shaped silhouette preying upon Africa

The Biblical Luke 21:9-19, put pen to paper about how a wicked husbandmen—*new ruler*—would gain power over the earth—vineyard. It reads: *"9. Then began he to speak to the people this parable; A certain man planted a vineyard, and let it forth to husbandmen, and went into a far country for a long time. 10. **And at the season he sent a servant to the husbandmen**, that they should give him of the fruit of the vineyard: **but the husbandmen beat him, and sent him away empty**. 11. And again he sent another servant: and they beat him also, and entreated him shamefully, and sent him away empty. 12. And again he sent a third: and they wounded him also, and* *cast him out. 13. Then said the lord of the vineyard, What shall I do? I will send my beloved son: it may be they will reverence him when they see him. 14. But when the husbandmen saw him, they reasoned among themselves, saying, This is the heir: come, let us kill him, that the inheritance may be ours. 15. So they cast him out of the vineyard, and killed him.* **What therefore shall the lord of the vineyard do unto them? 16. He shall come and destroy these husbandmen, and shall give the vineyard to others.** *And when they heard it, they said, God forbid. 17. And he beheld them, and said, What is this then that is written, The stone which the builders rejected, the same is become the head of the corner? 18. Whosoever shall fall upon that stone shall be broken; but on whomsoever it shall fall, it will grind him to powder. 19. And the chief priests and the scribes the same hour sought to lay hands on him; and they feared the people: for they perceived that he had spoken this parable against them".*

Clearly the vineyard represents the planet earth and the husbandman represents the temporary authority given to Yacub's grafted race whose rule over earth's original inhabitants and resources have been unmistakably evinced thus far. Then in verses {15} and {16} we see an ancient Christophany[65] concept indicating that God in Person is the only one who can and will put an end to the cabal of evil husbandmen and their global corruption. As one business executive expressed, "corruption is not a problem, it's a system".

In an earlier chapter, it was established that Islamic principles and sciences were taught to Europeans under the tutelage of the Berber Moors who conquered Spain (southern Europe) from the 7th – 11th century. And how these Muslims resurrected Europe out of a 500-year dark age. **Dark Ages** is a term in <u>historiography</u> referring to a period of cultural decline or <u>societal collapse</u>. Such history illustrates to us that Europe's

---

[65] A theophany is a manifestation of God in the Bible that is tangible to the human senses. In its most restrictive sense, it is a visible appearance of God in the Old Testament period, often, but not always, in human form.

Dark Age began with Rome's fall in the fifth century covering its continent wide chaos including raids by Vikings, Vandals and Visigoths, bubonic plague, famine, civil unrest and religious hypocrisy under the Popes of Rome.

Therefore, the tools employed by the Moors *(Black Muslims)* of Spain to help Europe move forward out of its dark age were Islamic textbooks of medicine, astrology, astronomy pharmacology, psychology, physiology, zoology, biology, botany, mineralogy, optics, chemistry, physics, mathematics, algebra, geometry, trigonometry, music, meteorology, geography, mechanics, hydrostatics, navigation and history. Many Arabic works were translated into Latin that facilitated the progress of science. But in return, how were the Moors repaid during the 14th century?

> *"Christians continued to re-conquer Spain, leaving a wake of death and destruction in their path. The books were spared, but Moor culture was destroyed and their civilization disintegrated. Ironically, it wasn't just the strength of the Christians that defeated the Arabs but the disharmony among the Moor's own ranks. Like Greece and Rome that proceeded them, the Moors of Al-Andalus fell into moral decay and wandered from the intellect that had made them great.*

> *"The translations continued as each Moorish haven fell to the Christians. In 1492, the same year Columbus discovered the New World, Granada, the last Muslim enclave was taken. Captors of the knowledge were not keeper of its wisdom. Sadly, all Jews and Muslims that would not abandon their beliefs were either killed or exiled (Grolier, History of Spain). Thus ended an epoch of tolerance and all that would remain of the Moors would be their books."[66]*

When European elitists, aristocrats, men of war, intellectuals and church leaders finally re-ordered their world, it was contrary to the order of the ancient scripture. Thus, corruption has become their system of Rulership. This is they have devised to rule by debt finance. By this I mean while Europe ultimately established and represented secularism

---

[66] www.xmission.com/~dderhak/index/moors.htm

throughout the globe, ancient aboriginal nations attempted to fight them by using ancient spiritual scripts as a guide to maintain world governance, trade and commerce free from usury viz., the worst form of corruption. But at the end of the day secularism became victorious.

What is secularism? Secularism asserts that governmental practices or institutions should exist separately from religion and/or religious beliefs and Western democracy came to pass. In another sense, secularism refers to a belief that human activities and decisions, especially political ones, should be based on evidence and fact unbiased by religious influence...The term "secularism" was first used by the British writer George Holyoake in 1846. Holyoake invented the term "secularism" to describe his views of promoting a social order separate from religion, without actively dismissing or criticizing religious belief...[67] Of course, secularism was absolutely contrary to all highly mechanized ancient civilizations of the Holy Land, Middle East and Near East before Caucasian rules of governance were thoroughly established.

Among the ancients, God's rule was the way. Each ruler was oftimes declared as man, ruler and god through which his governmental decisions were finalized after consulting with the Priesthood. In this manner, they were keeping with the tradition of ancient writings about the anthropomorphic divine being (God in Person) who was prophcied to come.

Ancient Black God

Ancient Hebrew's represented their God by writing four mysterious Hebrew letters (seen to your right). Religious scholar, Dr. Wesley Muhammad,[68] expounds these mysterious symbolic letters mean *"Lord"* representing the idea that the Black Man is God. These four letters are called Tetragrammaton and represent one of the names of the

---

[67] http://en.wikipedia.org/wiki/Secularism
[68] www.TheBlackGod.com for full understanding of Hebrew vertical letters.

anthropomorphic God of Israel. The name or symbol is sometimes referred to as the unvocalized Tetragrammaton since it contains no vowel points.[69]

Hebrew	Letter name YHWH
י	Yodh
ה	He (pronounced "hey")
ו	Waw
ה	He

Most modern denominations of Judaism teach the four-letter name of God, YHWH, is forbidden to be uttered except by the High Priest in the Temple. The name YHVH or YHWH is written with four consonants only; it is the holy Tetragrammaton, or in Hebrew, *Shem Hameforash*. Hebrew has no vowels. In ancient times, it didn't even have vowel points. These were added much later, and at that time pronouncing the name was already forbidden for generations. So no one knows how the most ancient name of God was pronounced. The vowel points make it sound like Yehova, and later it was anglicized to Jehovah. The reader may not say it. He or she must say instead the name Adonai, which means *"My Lord."* [70]

However, once upon a time, too publically say YHWH was nothing to speak of according to Ruth 2:4, *"And, behold, Boaz came from Bethlehem, and said unto the reapers, YHWH [be] with you. And they answered him, YHWH bless thee."* This strongly indicates that there was a time when the name was in common usage. I imagine though, it would be difficult for the Caucasian race to publically pronounce and acknowledge the

[69] http://en.wikipedia.org/wiki/Tetragrammaton
[70] http://www.pantheon.org/articles/y/yahweh.html

Black man as their maker if in fact that is what YHWH represents according to Dr. Muhammad's assessment.

"And God said, Let us make man in our image, after our likeness: and let them have dominion over the fish of the sea, and over the fowl of the air, and over the cattle, and over all the earth, and over every creeping thing that creepeth upon the earth." Genesis. 1:26

I ask might these four unvocalized symbols, *YHWH,* represent a hieroglyphic. Not in the exact form as the ancient Egyptian hieroglyphics, but an ancient Hebrew hieroglyphic to remind Yacub's made man of their maker— himself, a black man. Fact is early scholars purposed the meaning of *"Jacob-El"* to mean *"Jacob is my god."*[71] This idea would then be consistent with the Creator God, whom ancient Egyptian Priest referred to as Min. By this I mean ancient Egyptian Priest assigned the name **_Min_** to the Creator God as symbolized below in ancient Egyptian hieroglyphics. See next to Min how I have placed the Jewish holy Tetragrammaton, YHWH?

Min

The Creator-God (Khem or Min), is the god of reproduction; as Khnum. He was the creator of all things, *"the maker of gods and men"*. As a god of fertility (creator), he was shown as having black skin to reflect the fertile black mud of the Nile's inundation.[72]

With this awareness, the ruling monarch's of the Caucasian race viz., religious scientists, philosophers and financiers; in particularly during the formation of Europe, were

---

[71] http://www.bibleandscience.com/archaeology/exodus.htm
[72] http://en.wikipedia.org/wiki/Min_(god)

not to publically teach their laymen masses about ancient Black-God anthropomorphic theology. Had they divulged this degree of knowledge to the Western white world about the reality of their maker, Caucasian people would not have risen into power over the globe during their allotment of time to rule according to the nature in which they were created i.e. evil.

So beginning around 384 BC Aristotle's invisible God concept was instituted into Jewish and Christian religious theology. Aristotle's immaterial God concept was a sign of the times that an *anthropomorphic* Black God concept would not rule over the MIND of the white world's event horizon.

*"It is popularly assumed and even explicitly affirmed by Jewish and Christian theologians that God is an immaterial and formless spirit. Such an understanding of God does not derive from the Bible, but instead derives from later interpretations of this text. These later interpretations were influenced by Greek philosophy, particularly the ideas of the Greek philosophers Plato and Aristotle who are largely responsible for the development of the idea of an immaterial and formless deity. The God of the Bible in its original languages - Hebrew and Greek - is neither immaterial nor formless. Like the gods of the Ancient near east generally, the God of the Bible is **anthropomorphic**, that is to say he has a **form (morphe)** like that of a **man (anthropos)**. The very concept of an immaterial and formless deity was developed by the Greek philosophers who were repulsed by the anthropomorphic gods of the older Greek pantheon (circle of gods). The Ionian philosopher Xenophanes (570-475 BC) was one of the earliest to reject the anthropomorphism of the gods and argue that God should be characterized as non-anthropomorphic. Plato (428 - 348 BC) is pretty much the author of the very notion of 'immateriality'; before him it was recognized that all things, including spirit, was in some since material, even if that materiality was so subtle you could not see it. It was Plato's famous student, Aristotle (384-322 BC) who first explicitly applied this new concept of immateriality to God, his so-called "Unmoved Mover."*[73]

This changing of the guard in terms of establishing a worldwide neo-invisible God concept was initiated to empower

[73] http://www.truthofgodinstitute.com/Truth%20Of%20God%20Institute_files/index.html

the Caucasian race. By destroying the ancient Black God concepts and replacing them with a European self-image of God would assure the *Caucasians self-esteem* and *self-empowerment* in the realm of divinity. It would also instill within them the psychological advantage they'd need to overcome the darker skin nations but only for a season and for a reason. Thus we have the rationale behind the many images of Europe's God-Jesus concept.

| 6th Century Jesus | Modern Day Jesus | Leonardo da Vinci Jesus |

Simply put, if Yacub's grafted race were ever to usurp global authority in the allotment of time given to them (from year 9,000 to 15,000 Original Asiatic calendar) or (4086 BC to 1914 AD Christian calendar), kindness-alliances with ancient Black civilizations' had to be disrupted. All ancient Black God concepts were not to be followed according to the Biblical instructions provided to them by their maker, Yacub-El, except in secret.

*"And the children of Israel did evil again in the sight of the LORD, and served Buulim, und Ashtaroth, and the gods of Syria, and the gods of Zidon, and the gods of Moab, and the gods of the children of **Ammon** [Egypt], and the gods of the Philistines, and forsook the LORD, and served not him." (Jude 10:6)*

Many more verses such as these were provided to the leaders of the Caucasian race to serve only as a warning to prohibit them from worshipping that which once influenced the aboriginal mind and soul of the Holy Land. Therefore, when the first major invasions began around 3,500 years ago it generated vicious wars fought between Black and Caucasian (Aryan) or Sea people. Eventually as this new people began their lawlessness over the earth, dark skin people and their belief systems were demonized more and more.

Europe's men of war were programmed to even seek out and kill God in Person. This is how profound their Collegiums Pontificum—the most important priesthood of ancient Rome came to understand some of the ancient prophecies regarding the end times of their world's lawlessness of governance.

> *"4. ...Then the dragon stood before the woman about to give birth, to devour her child when she gave birth. 5. She gave birth to a son, a male child, destined to rule all the nations with an iron rod. Her child was caught up to God and his throne".* *(Revelations 12:3-5)*

Is God A Biological Reality

Not even the first Semitic or Red Arabs of 1,400 years ago could have accepted the idea of a Black Creator God because this degree of knowledge would have prevented their precincts from accepting ancient Islam's anthropomorphic God, Allah— The Divine Supreme Being. Therefore, Allah presented Himself in the Holy Quran as Light upon Light.

> *"Allah is the Light of the heavens and the earth.* **The Parable of His Light is as if there were a Niche and within it a Lamp:** *the Lamp enclosed in Glass:* **the glass as it were a brilliant star: Lit from a blessed** <u>**Tree, an Olive**</u>**, neither of the east nor of the west, whose oil is well-nigh luminous, though fire scarce touched it: Light upon Light!** *Allah doth guide whom He will to His Light: Allah doth set forth Parables for men: and Allah doth know all things. (Lit is such a Light) in houses, which Allah hath permitted to be raised to honour; for the celebration, in them, of His name: In them is He glorified in the mornings and in the evenings, (again and again),-"(Holy Quran 24:35-36)*

From my perspective, the meaning of this Quranic parable or metaphor above is very beautiful. It is a cryptic expression describing the reality of Allah as a Biological Reality—yet a Divine and Holy Man. For instance, *"His Light is as if there were a Niche and within it a Lamp: the Lamp enclosed in Glass: the glass as it were a brilliant star, Light upon Light."* In other words Allah is describing Himself in anthropomorphic terminology—as Anointed with Supreme Power contained within an integument or physical body. Next Allah says of Himself, *"Lit from a blessed*

Tree, an Olive, *neither of the east nor of the west, whose oil is well-nigh luminous, though fire scarce touched it: Light upon Light!* This means His roots or lineage and Supreme Wisdom has no beginning nor ending. Fact is this is the Holy One who appears in the last days as the Mahdi of the Muslim world and Messiah of the Christian world—God in Person. He says, *"neither of the east nor of the west"* because He is the answer for both worlds—original and grafted! The olive tree and its oil have even greater cultural importance as a religious element. For example: The verb *Meshach*-- from the same root word for *messiah* in Hebrew means *"to be anointed with olive oil."* Priests, kings and prophets were anointed with olive oil, indicating that they were gifted and called by God. So it was understood that the anticipated Messiah would be specially anointed with olive oil. The tree also represented the purpose of the promised Messiah to renew Israel.[74]

I think here it should be made clear: Of all the ancient rulers produced by the Original civilizations' particularly within ancient Egypt (who had declared themselves as gods and had idols fashioned into their images) none were to be worshipped by Yacub's race. But, the Anointed One, the Holy One whom the Honorable Elijah Muhammad declared he had met must be acknowledged by all nations including the Caucasian race. He was the ONE prophesied to come and indeed has come in the Personage of Master Wallace Fard Muhammad. In 1973 the Honorable Elijah Muhammad delivered a lecture expounding upon this truly Anointed One who indeed renewed the *captive* children of Israel—America's exslave descendants—Black America! The following words were transcribed from his lecture entitled "A Saviour is born."

As-Salaam-Alaikum...

In the name of Allah, The Most Merciful, To Whom Praise is due forever, The Lord of the worlds.

---

[74] http://www.susancanthony.com/AboutIsrael/Gethsemene.html

Brothers and Sisters, I'm so happy to see your smiling faces, who have come here from far and near to help us give thanks to Almighty God, Allah, Who came in the Person of Master Fard Muhammad, To Whom Praises is due Forever.

A Saviour's Day! Think about what we are here to worship. A Saviour's Day! Who is Lost that we had to have a Saviour's Day?

You may be seated.

I am a very happy man. A little small atom. I'm so small, you have to look for me, but if you keep your ears open, you will hear me. We have lots of people that is making our Saviour's Day Worship one of the most beautiful ones I ever saw. Coming in, we saw just a wall of our believers and our people that is seeking to learn what a Saviour's Day looks like. We have plenty people in this country, millions of them, that would be here if they understood, as you and me. Think over what day we say we are worshipping. A Saviour's Day!

We have been lost so long. Had been lost, excuse my English, so long that it has taken one that loved us. It has taken one that was made for us out of the two people to come and seek to find us and after finding us he had to have the power to save and deliver us.

This man had to be prepared. He was not already made and formed. He had to be prepared a form to get among us. He could not come as He was, in the spiritual form of the Nation's mind.

So His father had to prepare this man to come find us and then take us from our captors. We have to be taken. This is why that He, Himself, had to come. "Even I..." says the prophet, "...I will go after them. I will search the earth until I find them." A great lover with all power and with the eye to search the earth to locate that lost one.

We are a very beloved people, for God, Himself, to come and search the Earth and the Nations to find we that was lost. We are greatly beloved for God, Himself, to search the Earth for us. That's a beloved people.

He's so greatly in love His people that He threatened the whole population of the Earth to give them up. He said to me. He said that if you had been here in the days of Muhammad (may the peace and blessings of Allah be upon him) he would have come and gotten you himself.

That shows how important you are, that God will not allow one of us to be lost. Not say hundreds or thousands, but not one should be lost. He prepared Saviours to come for you. He says, in the Bible, "I will send Saviours after you."

If we are that important in the eyes of God and in the eyes of His angels that He will send Saviours. He will send a whole host of them after you. They shall gather you from the West and bring you. again, to your own.

This is the day. A Saviour's Day! One born on this day...Think over that!...to save this poor lost people that has been lost from their own over four hundred years. Going after them. "Even I", He says, "I will go". Not send, but "I'm going myself."

As some of us know that this has been practiced under secrecy, for a long time. But, today, He has arrived. Not King Solomon, but God, The King.

We are going to get over to you the History of This Man, Who is The Almighty God in Person, as He gave it to me.

He says to me, beginning His History -- that I want you to listen carefully to -- that His father was a Black man, very much so. And His mother was a white woman.

He said that His father knew he could not be successful in coming to a solid white country, and he being a solid Black man. So, He says to me, or rather He taught me, that His father said, 'I will go and make me a son. And I will send my son among them, looking like them.' Think over that!' And my son, they will think he is one of them. And He will find our lost people."

So Almighty God, in the Person of Master Fard Muhammad, says to me that he said, "I will have to make one look like them." So, He said, His father went up into the hills and there he found him a wife. A white wife. And he taken her and made a good Muslim out of her.

I don't know about that fancy that we have in the Bible that he cast seven devils out of the woman to make her fit for giving birth to This Man, The Saviour.

Now, I am not going to argue with no Theologian about it, because there is something in it to prepare a woman, that by nature, is born of the devil, to give birth to a Man destined to be the Ruler and God in Person, of the heavens and earth.

Naturally, he had to be careful in preparing his wife. (We have a very lot of this. You are not going to get through with this in fifteen minutes.)

So He says to me, or He taught me, that He was taken by His father, after He was born, and went looking for every good book or books that contained great words of wisdom spoken by great Kings and of all great people.

He said He would get a word or two for this one and a word or two from that one which was put away as a secret and he'd bring it and give it to Him. He paid the people high prices for such a word or two on the History of such-and-such man. So these things He was in preparation for a time.

Let's go back to the hills now. He says that after finding a wife for him in the hills. I am not going into that with you right now about where the hills were at and who was called the hill. I won't go into that with you right now. Some day you will hear me tell you but I want to be sure when I tell you this that the hills will welcome me to tell you.

We have from Him, He says to me, that His father married this woman and that the first child she birthed for him was a girl. And He said his father said, "Uhm, I missed that time!" So, He said, he made another try and that was Him. And, He said, he taken so carefully care of Him that He may be sent among the western people -- the Caucasian people. Of course, their real name you have known. Of course Caucasian is their name too. But their real name is the devil. But he needed one of these devil people in order to make complete...

This is not a mockery for me to stand here and call these people the devil because that's what they are. If any mockery should be done it should be done for us. If what we have made or created then the God of Blackman should be responsible for the mockery. I want to give you the truth. They didn't make themselves. We made them!

Well then, you have no right to be saying that your product is no good. Well if you made it no good then don't blame that which you made for being no good, because you made it. I know I'm coming to you in a way that you didn't think about. We are here to tell the truth.

As you have in the Epistles of Paul, in the Bible, he says there concerning this same subject. He says the clay said to the potter, "Why make me thus?" Well that's right! If you are the potter, the clay was innocent until you formed it and made it in something else. If you made another piece of pottery that you made mock of, you are the maker!

We must have understanding. We can't say that there was a mistake made and we should not recognize it. No. Listen at this good. I know you pretty well. The truth is truth. If one from among us made and enemy for us. Well we don't go after his product, for doing this, we go after the maker. Why did you make us an enemy? He replies back to us, "to show what was in you. He was in you and you didn't know it. So I brought him out of you and made a form to him." (We have got a lot of it. I think you are going to need some gloves to pat your hands).

So he made the white race by taking them from us. As the Holy Qur'an challenges them after they had been given the power to rule he reminds his creature, 'Don't forget who made you, was it you, yourself, or was it we that made you?"

This is to stop him from being proud over his maker, that he had something to do with it. We are the only created people on Earth. The Black man is a created man and the man that we call white, he is a made man from the Black man.

So since that the white race was made from the Black Nation -- the created people -- and now what was the purpose. It was the purpose to bring out of the Black man that which he didn't know that exists in him and that which existed in him could be made also ruler if given a form. And given the knowledge of the Black man, he could rule the Black man for a certain number of years until a greater one than he has been produced by the Black man.

So this is what our Saviour, Master Fard Muhammad found in us. Therefore, He came for us to save us because that we are people who belongs to the Creator. We are not a made people, as I repeat.

We are a created people. Therefore, getting after one that was created righteous, now, out of us this one created from us, an unrighteous people because we had that germ left in us from the creation of us. A germ that was not purified that it could not be changed into a wicked germ that we have in us today.

Another people -- a white people -- could be made from us today, as we stand now, regardless to how righteous we may be. We still contain the germ of unrighteousness. That is why we can do unrighteousness, because the germ is still there.

So, the great scientist went after it, by the name of Yacub. So he brought it out of us and gave the germ a form -- a body, then taught that form his wisdom and told this made man, that he made, "God forth, now, be faithful, work fast, you got six days to do all of your work and after that six days, the seventh day, The Brother coming from the East, he's gonna eat you up!"

I want you to get knowledge of This Saviour. That's what I'm working forward to. HIS purpose. HIS aims. This is what I am trying to get over to you. But I have got to bring you through history to get him to you.

He, Mr. Yacub -- the mighty scientist and maker of the white race or white man was no fool by no means, just because he made and enemy for us. This made us still great to know that in us was the germ of a whole race of people -- that we could form him and teach him then make him to rule the teacher, for a certain length of time, until the people produced one greater than he.

Now, today, this is our subject, today: 'A Saviour is born'. A Saviour out of the germ, out of the plunder -- out of the scrap human patch (We have got a lot of it), made out of that. Think over it.

He's made partly from the race of Yacub and partly from His own, just for the purpose to save you and me. A Saviour's Day is rightly called. That we are so beloved, we are so great a child out of the family of the Creator (Think over that!), who created the heaven and earth.

Should He let an enemy hold his child? Think over that! "No, I will go after him. Search My own earth for him and I will bring him, again, to Me."

'What you gonna do now, father?' 'I'm gonna clear this mistake so it will never happen again.' There will be, NEVER, a robbing or stealing away from our own, some of our people, by our enemies. No more! They won't be able to do so, for you are being taught the knowledge of the enemy and how can, now, he steals you after knowledge? How can he deceive you after knowledge? It cannot be done.

So, we were so beloved that God saw that He had to make a Saviour for us. In the Bible, it says, "He sent Saviour's after us. Think over that. Sent Saviour's -- lots of Saviours, to gather you from the hands of your enemy.

This has been a grieved thing. Just the idea that God has a child being held by an enemy, whom He has power over. Should He let them remain there, since there only is a few? No! Not even one! He will forgive you your sins and then save you from the hands of the enemy, who made you sin after they robbed you of the knowledge of self. Made you, then, to follow and obey them in evil so that they could have us for a mockery before the all wise and Holy God, Allah that you don't want to be like me. Oh no!

He has the power to take and forgive you because it is not a sin of ours. It's a sin that we were practicing because that we couldn't help ourselves from our enemies. We were reared up by enemies of ours and not friends. They deprived us of the knowledge of ourselves and of themselves. And when he made us dead to the knowledge of ourselves then he called us by his names. And, now, goes to war to keep you from getting into your own. Your own names. He don't want you 'Mr. Muhammad'. He wants 'Morehouse'. He wants 'Moore'. which is not a holy names. He calls you out of your name and calls you by his name. And as long as you go in his name, you belong to him. You will soon see in a few days. You come up with his name, you go with him. Because you rightly, then, belong to him, since that you refuse yourself and you're already in him then you go on to hell with him.

This race of people -- the white race -- was not made to be saved. Some of them will live, though, for a long time. Many centuries, those who have accepted Islam. There are many more of them that still awaits their turn to acknowledge Islam. They are coming into Islam, now, very fast, because they know the day they are living in and the time. You couldn't blame them. If I were in their place, you'd wake up looking at me and you would retire at night looking at me. I wouldn't ever leave your house, because this is a race of people to be destroyed and not to give them another chance on deceiving the people.

But there will be some that stick around maybe a thousand years. But they can't go beyond the thousand years, even if they have not or if they have believed, they can't go beyond the thousand years.

I won't go into no more of that, but that is true. But a man living here today that can hardly make it too far over fifty-four years old, he says that's okay with him if he can stick around that long -- a thousand years.

So let us not get away from our real subject of the making of a Saviour for us. Think over it, now. The Black man, He created heaven and earth and now comes to make a man. That's a small thing for Him to do, to make a man, when He'd taken one atom out of the total darkness of the universe and made Himself.

We should be happy that we are Black people! He made it so clear that He did not allow a child to be born unless that child is born out of total darkness. This is following up His Creation. Whether you are Black, white, red, brown or any color, you have got to be born out of total darkness to get on this side. So therefore, He made his word "Be" stand and steadfast. That we can't move about in the darkness nor light unless we give Him credit.

I want you to love Black because you are the universal God of all life. Regardless to what color it may be, originally it was made by Black man. There is no argument coming to you and me from the scientists of white people that you are not the original man of the Earth.

Their scientists know this because we have our mark on them. They couldn't deny it if they tried. If they know how to go into it.

We are the people to look forward to the....toward the making of heaven and earth, as we are going to do it. At least...I'm not saying I'm going to do it, but I'm helping now. This is why that you repeatedly hear something from the first. How it was done.

If you have caught up with the wisdom of that first man, then it needs a second man to change the whole thing around because you are not supposed to be standing aimless...No.

After the first God, we are practically, now, peeping into some of His artwork. And finding in the root of this artwork a way to change up the whole thing. This is why, again, that it is promised to you and me -- a new heaven and a new earth. Some of us say that is spiritually. Yes it is, at the present.

"Allah came to us from the Holy City Mecca, Arabia, in 1930. He used the name Wallace D. Fard, often signing it W.D. Fard. In the third year (1933), He signed His name W.F. Muhammad which stands for Wallace Fard Muhammad. He came alone."

"He (Mr. W.F. Muhammad, God in person) chose to suffer 3-1/2 years to show his love for his people, who have suffered over 300 years at the hands of a people who by nature are evil and wicked and have no good in them. He was persecuted, sent to jail in 1932, and ordered out of Detroit, on May 26, 1933. He came to Chicago in the same year and was arrested almost immediately on his arrival and placed behind prison bars.

He submitted himself with all humbleness to his persecutors. Each time he was arrested, he sent for me so that I might see and learn the price of Truth for us, the so-called American Negroes (members of the Asiatic Nation). He was well able to save himself from such suffering, but how else was the scripture to be fulfilled? We followed in his footsteps, suffering the same persecution.

My people are yet sound asleep to the knowledge of the good that is being carried for their deliverance."

Dr. Wesley Muhammad

Eastern Islamic scholars as stated earlier loath at the idea the Nation of Islam in the West promulgates that Allah (God) is a man. However, Islamic scholar, Dr. Wesley Muhammad (AKA True Islam) explains how and why Eastern Islamic scholars classified Allah (God) as an imperceptible or immaterial entity. He states this concept stems from a time around the 10th century AD when two elite Muslim groups; namely, Jahmiyya and

Mu'tazila were influenced under Greek religious philosophy. Dr. Muhammad states:

"Islam is considered the religion par excellence of divine transcendence. God, according to Muslim theologians, is absolutely 'Other.' He is immaterial, possesses no body or form, and invisible. This god, however, does not derive from the Qur'§n or Sunna, but derives from later Greek-inspired interpretations of the Qur'§n and Sunna.

"Like the God of the Bible, the God of the Qur'§n and Sunna is transcendently anthropomorphic: he has a human form, but one unlike that of man's in that it is dangerously luminous and eternal. The Qur'§n specifically describes God as a delimited being (shay', e.g. 6:19) with human physical characteristics (e.g. a face, two hands, eyes, leg, side, a soul, a spirit).

"The Sunna specifically refers to God as a person with a body (shakhs) and according to early 'orthodox' Sunni tradition God appeared to Muhammad in the form of a man (sh§bb). The early Muslims understood these passages to be literal descriptions of God. It was non-Sunni Muslim groups such as the Jahmiyya and Mu'tazila, influenced by Greek philosophy, who first rejected the anthropomorphism of the God of the Qur'§n and Sunna. Later, Islam's own 'philosophers' would work to bring the God of Islam in line with the god of Greek philosophy.[75]

Notice how the teaching of a mystery God was promulgated by the Aegean Sea people viz., Hellenistic Greeks. The term **Hellenistic** itself is derived from Ἕλλην (**Héllēn**), the Greeks' traditional name for themselves. Nevertheless, the Most Honorable Elijah Muhammad stated: *"According to Allah, the origin of such teachings as a Mystery God is from the devils! It was taught to them by their father, Yacub, 6,000 years ago. They know today that God is not a mystery but will not teach it. He (devil), the god of evil, was made to rule the nations of earth for 6,000 years, and naturally he would not teach obedience to a God other than himself.*[76]

---

[75] http://www.truthofgodinstitute.com/Truth%20Of%20God%20Institute_files/index.html
[76] http://www.muhammadspeaks.com/Mystery.html

Islamic scholars ascribing Allah as an imperceptible invisible being was codified under Greek Hellenism for intellectual, political and economical understanding and purposes.

"Another historical fact of encounter between Islam and the west took place in the wave of Hellenism as pointed by Montgomery Watt. Watt argued that Islam undertook three waves of Hellenism. The first and second wave of Hellenism struck when Islam interacted with the Greek philosophical ideas. Both waves were categorized as the pure intellectual wave of Hellenism. While the first wave was dominated by "imported" knowledge from Greek in the form of translation, the second one was an excellent synthesis between the atheist Greek philosophy with the monotheist Islamic philosophy."

"Meanwhile, the third wave of Hellenism was no longer intellectual interaction, but it penetrated into social, economic, and political scope. In the political and economic context, the third wave of Hellenism generated Islamic marginalization which makes them heavily dependent upon the west in the intellectual, political and economical context."[77]

Before Eastern Islamic people emerged into governments, Jews had been Hellenized under Greek culture in southern Europe (Mediterranean region) and Palestine. Prior to this time, their forbearers ascribed to the concept of an anthropomorphic Divine Being as mentioned in the Old Testament scriptures. So by the time Jesus (Isa) of 2,000 years ago was born, he had to contend with a Hellenistic world and Hellenistic Jews in the Middle East (Palestine) and parts of Europe because Hellenism swayed so much control over the Jewish population and white race in general. Thus Jesus (Isa Ibn Yusef) was made to say to a confused and hypocritical religious Jewish body-politic, *"Think not that I am come to destroy the law, or the prophets: I am not come to destroy, but to fulfill." (Matthew. 5:17)* But as the Honorable Elijah Muhammad was taught of Jesus, "He gave up his work of trying to convert the Jews or white race…" Jesus

---

[77] http://islamlib.com/en/article/islamic-reformation-and-the-myth-of-westernization/

discovered from the scripture that they had 2,000 more years to remain in the seat of power and authority.

Hellenism

Hellenistic civilization represented a fusion of the ancient aboriginal (Black) Etruscan Greek world with that of the Near East, Middle East and Southwest Asia, and a departure from earlier Greek attitudes towards "barbarian" cultures. The map to the right outlines the ancient Black Etruscan territory in what is now called northern Italy. It was through this aboriginal people that "pale skin Greeks and Romans" gained their ideas of building towns and cities, religion and science. The images below depict the first Etruscans.

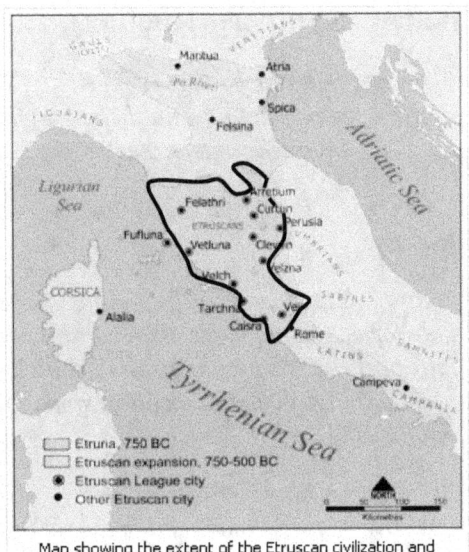

Map showing the extent of the Etruscan civilization and the twelve Etruscan League cities.

When the *pale skin Greeks* finally gained an upper hand of the Aegean/Mediterranean region, they grossly retold all of the stories taught to them by the dominate Black culture of the region whose settlements were founded by those whom *pale skin Greeks* refer to as Pelasgians and Etruscans. However, these aboriginal ancient Greeks were no more than offshoots of ancient Egyptians (Khemet).

"The fact that black kings from Africa were the first rulers of the Greek islands in the Aegean Sea and established civilization there is very well documented by the ancient Greek writers themselves.

"According to the Greek writer Herodotus who is also called the Father of History:

"How it happened that Egyptians came to the Peloponnese (southern Greece) and formed settlements there and what they did to make themselves kings in that part of Greece has been chronicled by other writers. I will therefore add nothing but proceed to mention some points, which no one else has yet touched upon.

"For example the names of nearly all the gods came to Greece from Egypt, moreover it was only, if I may so put it, the day before yesterday that the Greeks came to know the origin and form of the various gods ...for Homer and Hesiod, the poets who composed our theogonies and described the gods for us... lived as I believe not more than 400 years ago."—The Histories Book Two – Herodotus of Halicarnasus (circa 530 BC)

"The first settlements in the ancient Greek islands involving black colonists from Africa are generally attributed to a group called the Danaans or Danids. In ancient Greek and Roman poems and plays the Danids are explicitly described as being "black".

"According to the legends, the king Danaos had fifty daughters and his brother Egyptos had fifty sons. The brothers quarreled and Danaos and his daughters fled the North African coast by sea, hotly pursued by the sons of Aegyptos who wanted to marry the girls. Although the boys eventually caught up with them, the matter ended badly for the sons of Egyptos. After a forced mass wedding, their angry new wives killed all but one of the pursuers during the wedding night.

"Only one Danid daughter did not kill her new husband and they continued on as a married couple. It is from that union that the first kings and royal families of early Greece are said to have descended. They came to be known as the Heraklids (from Hercules) i.e. descendants of Danaan-Egyptian colonizers.

"Ancient Greek history also indicates how Danaos the father of fifty daughters on coming to Argos took up abode in the city of Inachos and throughout

Greece (Hellas) Danaos laid down the law that all people hitherto named Pelasgians were to be called Danaans.''[78]

As stated earlier, pale skin Greeks gained the upper hand and then retold and stole the legacy of the Black founders of the Aegean/Mediterranean region. Then 300 hundred years before the birth of Jesus, Jews and the white race in general came under the influence of a corrupted immoral life style of Greek culture.

*"Following the conquests of Alexander the Great (d. 323 BC), Judea (as Judah came to be called) passed under the rule of Alexander's Egyptian successors (the Ptolemies) and later his Syrian successors (the Seleucids). Under these Hellenistic rulers, Jewish life was changed both inwardly and outwardly, in Palestine and in the growing Diaspora. In Alexandria, which acquired a large Jewish population, novel forms of Judaism emerged. **The Bible was translated into Greek (the Septuagint),** the first of innumerable translations. New explanations of the Torah were devised in the 1st century AD by Philo of Alexandria.*

"The Greek language and customs also affected Palestinian Jewry; the Jewish emphasis on study may be in part the result of Greek influence. But while many Jews were attracted to pagan customs and attitudes, the majority resisted these trends. The attempt of the Seleucid king Antiochus IV to impose the Greek religion by force aroused open rebellion led by the Maccabees, a Jewish priestly family. During the short period of Judean independence under the Maccabees (also called Hasmoneans) a movement of proselytizing began that was apparently not organized but was nevertheless energetic. Large numbers of persons, disillusioned with the old pagan cults, adopted Judaism formally or attached themselves unofficially to the synagogue."

*"The worldliness of the later Maccabees alienated most of their subjects, and effective leadership passed more and more too pious and learned laymen, especially after the Romans established control in 63 BC. **These laymen formed the party of the Pharisees (separatists);** democratic in spirit, the Pharisees sought to adapt the laws of the Torah to changing needs, utilizing old popular traditions (oral Torah), which they expanded by the free method of Midrash, or*

---

[78] http://www.africaresource.com/rasta/articles/african-athena-and-the-modern-olympics/

*verse - by - verse interpretation of scripture. Their opponents, **the Sadducees, were drawn largely from the wealthy classes and from the priesthood; conservative in religious matters, the Sadducees interpreted scripture strictly, disregarding the oral tradition and popular customs, and rejecting the doctrine of resurrection.** The Pharisees were followed by the majority; all subsequent Judaism was pharisaic, and the roots of Christianity and Islam are found in pharisaic Judaism."*[79]

What ever the case might be, it was Pharisaic Judaism that rejected the message Jesus of 2,000 years attempted to establish among them. Could it have been due to what the scripture said, ***"Out of Egypt I have called my son."*** -- Matthew 2:15. What knowledge did Jesus gain in Egypt that was rejected by those whom were under the influence of Hellenism? Lastly, is it a coincidence that like Jesus, Moses was also taught the ancient wisdom of Egyptians?

Five Jewish Books

The primary five books of instructions for the Jews are Genesis, Exodus, Leviticus, Numbers, and Deuteronomy. These books are sometimes referred to as:

- the "*Five Books of Moses*," because the writings themselves identify the author as Moses, or
- the "*Pentateuch*," a Greek term meaning "*pente (5) teuchos (volumes)*," or
- the "*Books of the Law*", or
- the "*Torah*" (a Hebrew word meaning "*instruction*")

These books were originally written as a single unbroken scroll. Sometime before the 2nd Century BC it was divided into the 5 books that we see today.[80] As the European story is told, Moses provided these instructions to make sure Caucasians would get their chance to rule in the holy land. However, what they don't say is that these instructions derive from the mind of

---

[79] http://www.mb-soft.com/believe/txo/judaism.htm
[80] http://www.religioustolerance.org/chr_tora.htm

Black men, very wise men. So the scripture reads, *"Moses was educated in all the wisdom of the Egyptians and was powerful in speech and action." (Acts 22:7)* This indicates that Moses was permitted to teach some of the wisdom of ancient Egypt to the white race. It was this wisdom that gave them the capacity to rule and to establish monarchs and government systems.

Another major book of scripture provided to Caucasians is called Revelations. This book was written on the Isles of Pelan (Patmos), which is known as the Jerusalem of the Aegean—the holy island of Christians. Every Christian identifies with the Apocalypse (Bible book of Revelations) and believes St. John as its author. Except in reality, these books as well as the other five I mentioned actually contain portions of what Yacub provided to the Caucasian race before he died. He prepared their instructions while on Patmos over 6,000 years ago.

"The coming of the Mahdi as being One greater in knowledge and greater in wisdom than Yacub was seen and prophesied by Yacub and he prophesied His coming after him to destroy his civilization in Revelation."[81]

So therein the Book of Revelation 12, if you read beyond its symbolism, reveals how a special child would be born (an anthropomorphic being) to become Supreme in Power, Wisdom and Knowledge. Enough Power to finally end a wicked civilization that started out 6,000 years ago and grew into America and Europe during these end times even beyond Yacub's idea of civilization.

In 1947, the Honorable Elijah Muhammad was asked about Wallace Fard Muhammad and Yacub. His answer in short is as follows:

"First, we all are ALLAH, but MASTER W.D. FARD MUHAMMAD is SUPREME over all of us is referred to all times as the SUPREME BEING. He is SUPREME over all other beings, because HIS WISDOM, KNOWLEDGE, UNDERSTANDING and POWER to destroy and reproduce and create another Universe or make a people, makes HIM GREATER than

---

[81] http://www.muhammadspeaks.com/TheBeastwitheyes.html

all, and is WISER than those before HIM even He who created this Universe, because this ONE is able to reproduce or destroy it, or bring in one better, so says the Holy Quran.

"Who was ALLAH Before MASTER W.D. FARD MUHAMMAD was born? Who was ALLAH when Jesus was born?

"Now there are twelve (12) Imams or Scientists, who have been ruling all the time, and one of the twelve is always greater than the other eleven (11), but the God of this world before the birth of Jesus and up until 1877 was Yacub. That means that the God of this world, Yacub, although he lived only 152 years, has ruled for the last six thousand (6,000) years; therefore, he was in power when Jesus was born, and that is why Jesus wasn't able to set up His Kingdom, because the wicked God's time was not up.

" A people who have been taught that the SUPREME BEING is other than a Being, something spooky-like, it is not so easy for them to see out of that dark and ignorant teaching into reality."

The man Yacub was a God. He is known as Kronos according to Greek mythology. He made the white race on Isles

of Patmos (Pelan) shown above.

CHAPTER 12

Black Power Movement

The term Black power is most often attributed to the Black Panther Party of the 1960's. This organization of black men and women advocate that black people must organize themselves into a nation employing self-determination. In fact during the 1980's while standing post, I recall seeing the *new Black Panther* leader, Attorney Malik Zulu Shabazz, often seated at Muhammad's Mosque # 27 Los Angeles California listening to lectures delivered by the late Dr. Khalid Abdul Muhammad, former  national representative of the Honorable Minister Louis Farrakhan Muhammad.

The idea of Black Power must not be shunned by anyone with good sense. The Honorable Elijah Muhammad said *"that Black, by itself, is no color. It is original. It is not from any other color. It is durable in any climate of the earth and it remains the same."*

Then he asked to question: <u>How Independence is born</u>? When a people is smart enough to look and dig into the earth and get what she produces, her secret treasures hidden under the surface, along with her water, air, and sunshine, that people can be self-supporting as other smart nations are who are, independent of each other.

Some may have in their part of the earth that which the other does not have and next comes the exchange of resources to others through peaceful means, a trade and exchange of goods with each nation. Only disagreement and war and fighting between each other would prevent such necessary union of Nations to get that from the other nations that she does not produce.

A new nation should not isolate itself from national or international trade. However, this does not mean mixing blood with each other. The borders of a black and white separate state should be as strict as any nation's borders, protected by passports and visas for all people, think the so-called Negroes and white Americans should have such restrictions and laws between them to maintain peace. Intelligent Will Agree. I do believe the intelligent minds of America would agree to the separation of us into some place other than trying to continue making us live with them with the same respect and justice that they enjoy not to mention the mixing of bloods and the complete care of us. If they see you and me in honest togetherness on some of this earth that we can call our own, even with some help as Egypt did for Israel on Israel's departure, they will respect us.

Would we get along in peace if we were put together to live together? Answer: I know we would, if our national religion would, be ISLAM; this I am proving to you daily. See how peacefully my followers and I get along together? It is God in the religion of Islam who inspires love, unity and peace in the hearts and actions of every true believer. Once you accept Islam, you do not even like to dispute and quarrel with the brothers or sisters. Allah will soon put Islam in the hearts of all the lost-found Muslim in America to share with them, if others fail. It is a Must that we be separated into some part of this earth that we can call our own.

Next, do we have the qualified men and women among the black people of America to run a nation? [82]

The answer to the above question will only be exemplified through action from all black people' throughout the four corners of the globe working together in the best spirit. Bickering and debating over how to unify black men, women and children is only a trap of the enemy from within and without. It is best that Africa and Black America unite as the

---

[82] www.muhammadspeaks.com/thetruth4-5-1962.htmlgovernment for self ?

globe is turning and waiting on no one to understand the power of unity.

Build Black Economy

BLACK ECONOMY is one of the first steps that is necessary for the BLACK MAN to take; FROM ECONOMY IN HIS HOME to farms and factories.

WE BOAST that we are free. To boast of FREEDOM OF SELF, means that you are one who is responsible for your economic condition. A PEOPLE dependent upon another people to take your responsibility means that you are putting yourself in the position to be a SUBJECT PEOPLE, to another people, who are free.

IF WE LOOK FORWARD to our slave-masters, to teach us economy, it may prove a failure in the end, unless they are friends of ours, instead of our open enemies.

THE WHITE AMERICANS have proved themselves to be our open enemies. If we watch them in order to learn their way of economy, we will become a most extravagant people. AMERICA, who has become the most wealthy people on the face of the earth, is also one of the most extravagant and wasteful people on the earth.

SO, WE THE BLACK PEOPLE, the once-slave and now a SUBJECT PEOPLE should not try to adopt the economic ways of a people who cannot truthfully say that they practice economy, among themselves. THEREFORE, America produces a slave who is also extravagant, with what little he gets. He has his eyes and mind set upon obtaining aid from his extravagant master. He hopes to be, in time, just like his master. Since he has never had any other master or guide than his slave-master, he imitates his master.

HIS SLAVE-MASTER keeps him down, by not caring to teach him economy. As long as the once-slave tries to practice to be the equal of his master, before he ever learns and practices SELF-ECONOMY, the slave-master will always keep him in want, because of such extravagant ideas. CERTAINLY WE WANT WEALTH. We cannot enjoy life without wealth, but we should economize that wealth until we are equal with other nations in the way of economics.

LIVING UNDER and TAKING AS AN EXAMPLE, one of the most rich and powerful governments on earth, should give us a good lead toward self, in the way of wealth. With this wealth economized, the slave should emerge very powerful, for himself.

WHITE AMERICANS (some of them), offer help to us. But it is disgusting to the teacher to find that when he looks back, he sees that you are not practicing economics. THERE ARE SOME WHITE PEOPLE WHO hate to see the once-slave bending under the yoke, and they are sincere. But, be careful in accepting help from a tricknologist who would like to trick you into a worse state, by pretending friendship, for you.

THE BEST BLACK BUSINESS AND POLITICAL MINDS of our people need training into the KNOWLEDGE of SELF and the future, FOR SELF.

STOP TRYING to be OTHER THAN YOUR OWN SELF. Do not depend on OTHER THAN YOU OWN SELF for your BLACK FUTURE. DEPENDING on SELF TODAY will keep you from making grave mistakes TOMORROW. WE MUST NOT depend on SELF for help, WE MUST DEPEND ON THE HELP OF ALLAH (God).

THE ABOVE SAID business and political minded of our people, being without the KNOWLEDGE of SELF and how to BUILD the most proper and successful ECONOMY among the BLACK MAN, is due to his being proud of what the white slave-master has taught him, of himself.

THIS TEACHING from the slave-master is designed to always keep him SUBJECT to the slave-master's children.

WE NEED TERRITORY IN WHICH TO EXPAND. We need some of this GOOD EARTH here or there so that we can BUILD a SYSTEM of ECONOMY.

YOU, MR. POLITICIAN AND MR. PROFESSOR, are so willing to stay under the official shelter of the business and political white man, that you have very little love and mercy for the tens-of-millions of your own people out here, trying to suck blood out of a turnip.

CREATE IN YOUR OWN HEART, love for your own people, who are wallowing in the mud and who are suffering from hunger and lack of shelter.

THE BIBLE PROPHECY, relating to the PROFESSIONAL Black once-slave, is very sad. Even their spiritual leaders, the preachers are denounced by Jesus, in his prophecy. Bible Is. Chap. 56, Matt. 23:13. WE MUST TRY TO BEAT this prophecy if we can. THIS IS WHAT I AM TRYING TO DO.

DO NOT GET THE IDEA of robbing the ALREADY ROBBED Black People, just because you have learned HOW to rob them from the teachings of the slave-master and his children. THIS IS ONE OF THE HABITUAL practices on the part of the PROFESSIONAL CLASS, of our people.

IF YOU MAKE THE LABORER WEALTHY, he is still in your orbit and you share in it. HE WILL LOVE AND HONOR you if you enable him to become SELF-SUFFICIENT. I SPEND ALL OF MY TIME,

NIGHT AND DAY, trying to do just this one thing...raise a FALLEN and DEAD people, to their feet, so that they may GO FOR SELF and BUILD FOR SELF, but not on the pattern of his slave-master which is robbery, spoiling, and corruption of each other.

COME ALONG WITH ME, if you would love to BUILD an ECONOMIC SYSTEM for our people under the name BLACK, which is adopted from me, by you, for the last few years.

I have been PREACHING BLACK for about 39 years. IF YOU ARE GOING TO TEACH MY TEACHINGS and FOLLOW ME, in the teachings of BLACK and BLACK DOING FOR BLACK, it would be wise of you to go along with me, while you have only YOURSELF.

YOURSELF, Alone, Will Not Work Against The POWERFUL FORCE Which Is Against You. YOU MUST HAVE DIVINE HELP And NATIONS OF YOUR KIND, With You. I Have These Things.

COME LEARN FROM ME, And Do Something GOOD For Our People, Instead Of Robbing Our People, Under A Name...BLACK. THAT IS LIKE TRADING THE LION FOR A WOLF.[83]

Africa To America

Slavery was well established in the **New World** (Americas) by the Spanish, Portuguese, and Dutch, who all sent African slaves to work in both **North and South America during the late sixteenth and early seventeenth centuries.** The English began aggressively trading in what was called "black ivory" [which], spurred on by the need for laborers in the hot, humid sugar fields on the West Indian islands of Barbados, St. Christopher, the Bermudas, and Jamaica. Like other European nations, England created the [Royal African Company] to underwrite the slave trade. A string of forts and 'slave factories' were established from the Cape Verde Islands to the Bight of Biafra. But the slave trade would likely not have been as 'successful' were it not for the 'unholy alliance' between the English (and other European nations) and the African kingdoms on whose territories the forts stood.

---

[83] http://www.muhammadspeaks.com/Economy.html

The English slave traders did their best to dupe the native kings, and each native king did his best to obtain the maximum amount of goods in exchange for the slaves he had for sale.[84]

Often times when one engages in a good conversation with elderly Black Americans about slavery, you hear them proudly express how they are glad the white man brought *"us"* to America and how we are better off in America than in Africa. In fact, this idea might even be fixed into the far mental resesses of many young Black youth too. Although they will not agree with slavery, segregation etc; America is considered HOME wherein many Black people yet strategize to overcome institutionalized anti-Black practices, micro and macro racism!

Then on the other hand, if one were to convey how Black America fulfilled Abraham's prophecy during the 16th, 17th, 18th and 19th century as slaves in a strange land 400 years *(Genesis 15)*; it only goes into one ear and out of the other ear. African American slave history does not compute with today's reality. Far too many do not relate America's slave historiography to Biblical prophecy lest it concerns the 2,000 and 4,000 year old struggles with respect to Caucasian people. What a shame….Nevertheless if Black America has fulfilled Abraham's seed, the question becomes: Why did God want them in a strange land under Caucasian rule and authority as slaves for 400 years or more.

Caucasian peoples' evil history in North America and throughout the entire globe for that matter is very difficult to

[84] http://sciway.net/hist/chicora/slavery18-2.html

phanton not only by modern day African American youth but many young white Americans wonder why their forefathers were so evil, vile and wicked toward dark skin people.

Although American and European historians will not admit exactly when the first African slaves were brought to North America and conquered; they do agree that the first slaves were brought to America from Southwest Africa, Angola.

Let us just say, thank Allah (God) that Europe and America's evil religious right-wing have not the authority it once exercised in judgment of the darker skinned nations of the globe. The Black Nation shall arise! Although they are slow to unite, they are sure to unite.

Oprah Goes To South Africa

In 1652, the Dutch East India Company founded Cape Town. Cape Town became a British colony in 1806. European settlements expanded during the 1820s as the Dutch, Flemish, German and French settlers and the British settlers claimed land in the north and east of the country. Conflicts arose among the Original nation and grafted race that competed for territory. The originals were subdued.

Later the discovery of diamonds and later gold triggered a conflict between Caucasian-Anglos and Caucasian-Boers. These two groups fought for the control of the South African mineral wealth and to control the trade routes to India that passed around the Cape. Although the Boers were defeated,

Boers

the British gave limited independence to South Africa in 1910 as

149

a British dominion. In the Boer republics and subsequent South African governments, the system became legally institutionalized <u>segregation</u> known as *apartheid*, otherwise known as anti-blackism.

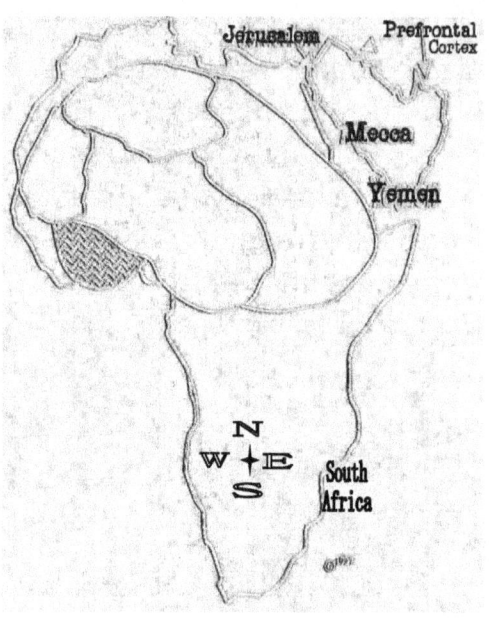

The Original nations lose of South Africa to Caucasians was quite a blow to the Mother continent. It was as if she took a final knockout punch to the jaw. In fact, looking at the skull shaped continent, notice South Africa is her lower jaw. In human anatomy, the lower jaw is at least partly responsible for a lot of knock-outs during a fight. When one gets hit on the point of the chin, the jawbone slams back against the nerve, basically causing a form of sensory overload—knock out! Contact on the point of the chin is not unlike any other contact to the skull vault that shakes the brain and can create either a quick knockdown or knockout. However, the human head can take some amazing contacts of varying force without getting knocked out. Any hit to the jaw is potentially damaging to the joint itself and the skull cavity.

The question becomes: When South African Blacks truly awaken, will it ignite Africa's MIND for Continental Unity?

A meeting between Oprah Winfrey and Nelson Mandela was merely sign of the revival of the Black nation. This process begins with EDUCATION of the highest order! By this I mean, during the meeting with Nelson Mandela, Ms. Winfrey said:

"...she decided to build the academy in South Africa rather than the United States out of <u>love</u> and respect for Mandela and because of her own African roots.

"She said she planned a second school for boys and girls in the eastern province of KwaZulu-Natal.

"Many state-funded schools, especially in the sprawling townships that sprang up under white racist rule, are hopelessly overcrowded and lack even basic necessities such as books.
"They also are plagued by gang violence, drugs and a high rate of pregnancy among school girls.

"Top-class study and sporting facilities are available, but are largely confined to private schools that are still dominated by the white minority as they are too expensive for many black and mixed race South Africans."[85]

The following structures depicted on the next page were built by indigenous South African people between 1250 AD and 1450 AD; believed to be the ancestors of modern Zimbabweans. South Africa's remarkable ruins of Zimbabwe only demonstrate inklings into the engineering mindset of South African people. Her ancient ruins were constructed without mortar. Their visual effect is spellbinding and reminiscent of the stone hand fitted fences of Zacatecas in Mexico.

[85] http://www.msnbc.msn.com/id/16435995/

These ruins of Great Zimbabwe are lofty, majestic, awe-inspiring and timeless. The quality of the building in places is outstanding. Craftsmen some proclaim by the Lemba people who took a pride in their work built it. In any event, there is nothing to compare with it in southern Africa.

From East, North, West and South the Original black nation has left their mark on the entire globe. Now the time has arrived for them to unite as one United Continent of Africa rooted in freedom, justice, and equality. To demonstrate and complete the laws of moral, ethical, legal, social conduct and all other matters of significance for humanity at large is their divine mission.

Bibliography

1. Dr. Richard Rastak M.D. Pg. 152 (1984)

2. African Presence in Early Asia, by Ronoko

Rashidi and co-edited by Ivan Van Sertima: Pg. 287 (1985)

3. African Presence in Early Asia, by Ronoko

Rashidi and co-edited by Ivan Van Sertima: Pg. 276-278 (1985)

4. Dr. Richard Rastak M.D. Pg. 10 (1984)

5. Great Pyramid Decoded, by E. Richard Capt. Pg. 8 (1971)

6. www.ashp.cuny.edu/slavetrade.html

7. Muslim Spain and European Culture (Burke, 1985, p. 42)

Acknowledgment

I thank all whom have posted magnificent images through the public domain of today's Internet whereby I was able to find by input nearly 90 descriptions of places, persons and maps that aided me to enhance the words of this book. Truly; as quoted by the 18th century Russian writer <u>Ivan Turgenev</u>, *"A picture shows me at a glance what it takes dozens of pages of a book to expound."*

www.ingramcontent.com/pod-product-compliance
Lightning Source LLC
Chambersburg PA
CBHW081352280526
45788CB00009B/2849